Merchants *in the* City of Art

Merchants *in the* City of Art

WORK, IDENTITY, AND CHANGE IN A FLORENTINE NEIGHBORHOOD

ANNE SCHILLER

Teaching Culture: UTP Ethnographies for the Classroom

UNIVERSITY OF TORONTO PRESS

LIBRARY AND ARCHIVES CANADA CATALOGUING IN PUBLICATION

Schiller, Anne (Anne Louise), author
   Merchants in the city of art : work, identity, and change in a Florentine market / Anne L. Schiller.

(Teaching culture : UTP ethnographies for the classroom)
Includes bibliographical references and index.
Issued in print and electronic formats.

ISBN 978-1-4426-3462-6 (bound).—ISBN 978-1-4426-3461-9 (paperback).—ISBN 978-1-4426-3464-0 (pdf).—ISBN 978-1-4426-3463-3 (html).

   1. Markets—Italy—Florence. 2. Merchants—Italy—Florence. 3. Vendors and purchasers—Italy—Florence. 4. Globalization—Italy—Florence. 5. Ethnology—Italy—Florence. 6. Florence (Italy) —Economic conditions. 7. Florence (Italy)—Social conditions.
I. Title. II. Series: Teaching culture.

HF5474.I8S35 2016 381'.180945511   C2015-905654-3   C2015-905655-1

We welcome comments and suggestions regarding any aspect of our publications—please feel free to contact us at news@utphighereducation.com or visit our Internet site at www.utppublishing.com.

North America
5201 Dufferin Street
North York, Ontario, Canada, M3H 5T8

2250 Military Road
Tonawanda, New York, USA, 14150

ORDERS PHONE: 1-800-565-9523
ORDERS FAX: 1-800-221-9985
ORDERS E-MAIL: utpbooks@utpress.utoronto.ca

UK, Ireland, and continental Europe
NBN International
Estover Road, Plymouth, PL6 7PY, UK
ORDERS PHONE: 44 (0) 1752 202301
ORDERS FAX: 44 (0) 1752 202333
ORDERS E-MAIL: enquiries@nbninternational.com

Every effort has been made to contact copyright holders; in the event of an error or omission, please notify the publisher.

This book is printed on paper containing 100% post-consumer fibre.

The University of Toronto Press acknowledges the financial support for its publishing activities of the Government of Canada through the Canada Book Fund.

Printed in the United States of America.

ai fiorentini di origine, naturalizzazione o affezione

CONTENTS

ILLUSTRATIONS

ACKNOWLEDGMENTS

Legend tells of a novel plan devised by the Republics of Florence and Siena to resolve a boundary dispute. At cock's crow, each would dispatch a horseman. The boundary would fall wherever the two horsemen met. For the sake of fairness, the Republics also agreed to exchange roosters. In Siena, the Florentine rooster enjoyed the city's usual hospitality, whereas the Florentines put the Sienese cock in a miserable coop with nothing to eat. The Sienese rooster was so unhappy that it began crowing even before sunup, and the Florentine Republic's horseman raced out in the dark. Unfortunately for Siena, the contented Florentine rooster overslept. By the time it crowed and the Sienese horseman could depart, Florence had already secured much new territory. The lesson, Florentine friends say, is that Florentines are excellent strategists but poor hosts.

I personally have never found Florentine hospitality lacking. Spending time in that remarkable city and coming to know some of its residents have been among my life's greatest privileges. Acquaintances, colleagues, and friends there and elsewhere in Italy have assisted me in many different ways, all of them indispensable. There are too many to mention each individually. Still, I would like to offer special thanks to Antonio Allegretti, Roberto Ambrocini, Dario Anforini, Stephanie Ball, Maria Grazia Belardini, Viola Belli-Blanes, Marcello Bellini, Maurizio Benvenuti, Fabio Borghi, Roberto Calamai, Giovanni Capuano, Carlo Cecconi, Cassandra Ciabani, Massimo Ciampi, Pietro Clemente, Lana Cunha, Marcello D'Ercole, Sandra Di Biasi, Haritan Diga, Ennio Fellinni, Elena Ferri, Elena and Francesco Folli, Maria Fusco, Nikol Gaggioli, Michelangelo and Massimo Galami, Luca Giovanelli, the Guerri family, the La Regina family, Silvia Lelli, Giancarlo Lombardi, Lidia Loschiavo, Aurelia Manfredi, Renato Manni, Marina Martin, Mariagrazia Messina, Marcello Monnetti, the Ortis family, Luciano and Fedora Radicchi, Beatrice Romano, Francesco Caglia Saverio, Alessandro Savorelli, Ali Shahrestani, Alessandro Sieni, MD Nejam Uddin

Sarker, Sabrina Stianti, Dragos and Giulia Tanasoiu, Roberto Tito, Camilla Torna, and Alessandro Viviani. Thank you to Steve Kalar for permission to include an image of his oil painting "Purple Flower."

Fabrizio and Carla Guarducci are untiring neighborhood advocates who have helped me in many ways. Milva Porfidio and Luca Casaglia offered assistance from my first day in Florence in 1999 and helped secure my marketplace apprenticeship. Anna Paola Baldini is an incisive cultural observer and model friend. She has supported me by critiquing drafts, assisting with points of translation, keeping an eye on the local newspaper, and more. *Grazie di cuore.*

I am indebted to Alessandro, Silvia, Silvano, and Silvana Belli-Blanes for the opportunities, trust, and warmth they have extended to me. A successful and entrepreneurial family, they have been fixtures and good neighbors in San Lorenzo for decades. I am fortunate to count them among my close friends. *Vi sono profondamente grata.*

I have studied Italian with many excellent teachers, but I offer particular thanks to a dear friend, Maddalena Mathis Boyer. I am grateful to the North Carolina State University Office of Undergraduate Research for funding made available to students involved in this project. North Carolina State University students contributed much as field assistants. Thanks to Caroline Chamblee, Amy Cowhig, Devki Gharpur, Christina Gordon, Sarah Kim, Daniel Shattuck, Gunasehare Shunmugamm, and Alexandra Wiedeman. Christopher Hutton, also an NC State undergraduate student, assisted as field photographer. Steven Harris-Scott and Zayna Bizri served as my graduate research assistants at George Mason University and lent their scholarly talents to the project during much of the writing period. Field research was supported, in part, by a Faculty Development Grant from North Carolina State University. Dr. Peter Stearns, now Provost Emeritus at George Mason University, generously accommodated follow-up trips to the field. I am grateful to Ms. Anne Brackenbury and Dr. John Barker of the University of Toronto Press for their guidance, and to anonymous manuscript reviewers for constructive suggestions.

My parents, John and Frances Schiller, and aunt, Dorothy Myers, have encouraged and supported me throughout the years. I would never have visited San Lorenzo were it not for Matthew Zingraff. His scholarly insights strengthened every stage of this project, and his companionship made for the happy circumstances in which I completed them.

Those who endeavor to communicate what they have observed in their travels have sympathy for the predicament that Dante Alighieri described in his masterwork, *The Divine Comedy*: "*Da quinci innanzi il mio veder fu maggio che 'l parlar mostra, ch'a tal vista cede, e cede la memoria a tanto oltraggi.*" All translations, omissions, and errors in this book are my own.

CHAPTER ONE

SAN LORENZO NEIGHBORHOOD AND ITS GLOBALIZED MARKET

Florence, *Firenze*, capital of Tuscany and birthplace of the Italian Renaissance, is a celebrated city. It was declared a World Heritage Site in 1982, and the United Nations Educational, Scientific, and Cultural Organization (UNESCO) describes the historic center as "a treasure chest of works of art and architecture."[1] American writer Mark Twain credited the city with the ability "to stir the coldest nature and make a sympathetic one drunk with ecstasy" (Smith 2010: 245). British poet Elizabeth Barrett Browning praised it as "the most beautiful of the cities devised by man" (Kenyon 1899: 331). It boasts pride of place on lists of the world's most beautiful cities, and approximately two million visitors respond annually to its siren call. In addition to taking in remarkable museums, churches, and other sites, many travelers seek experiences they associate with an Italian lifestyle. Shopping in local markets falls squarely among such experiences.

One of Florence's best-known marketplaces is located in a neighborhood called San Lorenzo. Thousands of shoppers frequent the San Lorenzo Market (*Mercato di San Lorenzo*) nearly every day. A vast array of merchandise and fresh meat, fish, and produce is artfully displayed for inspection in hundreds of stands and small shops. Greengrocers hand out succulent blackberries and toothsome chunks of cantaloupe to passersby. Vendors and customers engage in lively discussions of workmanship, materials, quality, and price. Shoppers frequently walk away with a token from a merchant tucked in their bag: a bunch of herbs to flavor a broth, a fresh-baked breadstick, or perhaps a Pinocchio pencil for a well-behaved child. Promotional leaflets from the 1990s suggested that the colorful market stands recalled painting exhibitions, although the market's true spectacle was buyers and sellers mutually engaged in a true and real symphony of sound and racket.

---

1 For more information, see the "Historic Center of Florence" entry in the UNESCO World Heritage List at http://whc.unesco.org/en/list/174.

To reach this market in the heart of the city, eager shoppers or curious tourists take several routes. For example, a few steps from the stunning green and white marble baptistery in front of Florence's cathedral is a street called Borgo San Lorenzo, the quickest route to the San Lorenzo Church and the market from this direction. Those coming from a few blocks north can cross via XXVII Aprile and head down Saint Zanobi or Saint Reparata Streets. Those who arrive by train can simply walk up National Street, make a quick right turn onto Silver Street, and reach the market within five minutes. To paraphrase a famous saying, almost all roads, and several alleyways, lead to San Lorenzo, as those who have visited or will visit already know or will find out.

Whatever road you choose, you are part of a surging crowd made up of stylish city residents talking on cellphones, uniformed construction workers repairing streets and renovating buildings, tourists with suitcases and water bottles, visiting businesspeople armed with leather portfolios, and assorted others. Along with everyone else, you navigate along narrow stone sidewalks, step into busy streets jammed with Fiats, BMWs, and Vespas, and maybe stop occasionally to window shop. Even if the market is your final destination, the small stores that beckon from ground floors of many San Lorenzo buildings offer constant temptation if you are inclined to indulge your consumer instincts or simply enjoy a blast of air conditioning or heat.

If you find yourself in San Lorenzo in the early morning, your sense of smell and appetite are stimulated by the fragrance of *espresso* and freshly-baked *cornetti* pastries, the "little horns" sometimes filled with jam or chocolate, wafting from coffee bars. You see vendors hurrying to get their merchandise to market in tiny three-wheeled delivery trucks or on carts. By midday the dominant aromas are of roast pork and pizza, though there may also be a hint of catalytic converter in the air. In warmer months, restaurants permitted to do so set up outdoor tables, all of which are likely to be occupied, with long lines of diners hungrily waiting their turns nearby. The crowds are back at dinner time, which Florentines jokingly note is 6 pm for North Americans and later for everyone else.

When you arrive at the market itself, you encounter a scene that is at once similar to and different from all you have observed before. Rather than hundreds of people walking swiftly down the street, you see them ambling among outdoor carts or standing alongside them. When you find yourself at the top of the Central Market building's staircase, automatic doors glide open to facilitate your entrance into an interior space rich with color and commotion. Indoors and out you hear people chatting with one another in lexicons reminiscent of the United Nations. It is fascinating to watch a Korean shopper interacting with an Italian vendor, both searching for the right English word to facilitate their transaction, or to see a

Florentine customer's pleasant surprise when a foreign merchant conducts their interaction in perfect Italian. As at the United Nations, too, you find yourself face-to-face with people from all over the world, distinguished by their accent, dress, comportment, and, as this book shows, their reason for being there in the first place.

San Lorenzo has lately become known as much for the diversity of the people who shop and work in it as for the variety of goods on sale. It is a highly contested site, in part because it is the protagonist of a saga that revolves around how identity and heritage may be portrayed and operationalized in a changing urban neighborhood. How to improve livability and preserve heritage in San Lorenzo are hot-button issues. The proposition that drives this book is that San Lorenzo is more than simply an interesting place to shop. It is an opportune setting in which to investigate some of the ways in which globalization, in particular transnational migration, has affected a population known for its mercantile skill, in a city beloved by millions.

The story about stability and change that is told in this book is being played out through multiple actors, some more evident than others, in a single place over a few generations. Each affects and is affected by this market and what goes on in it. The setting is an everyday work environment where commercial and social encounters make San Lorenzo what it is. The actors include vendors, residents, day laborers, the public, tourists, civic officials, and forces of politics and economics. A specific group of ambulant vendors, mostly Florentine by birth, is foregrounded. The book examines how they earn their living while dealing with what they perceive as new challenges to their identities as merchants and/or as Florentines. Their situation, however, goes beyond a nostalgic and perhaps idealized reminiscence of how things used to be in the face of new realities. Many of these vendors, some of whom have been working in the same two-by-three-meter spot for decades, interpret the changes around them as threats to a Florentine way of life. They view new increases in the numbers of new-immigrant–licensed vendors and illegal vendors as boding poorly for the marketplace's traditional tone and character; their concerns in this regard revolve around how vendors comport themselves. At the same time, they also worry that the security of their livelihood—that is, their continued ability to work as ambulant vendors—is increasingly at risk.

For some others in San Lorenzo and this city, however, the challenges facing San Lorenzo are more often seen as resulting from the market's increased size in general, and, more specifically, from the apparent intensification of incivility that has accompanied this growth. From that perspective, current realities present opportunities for the market's overhaul, perhaps even a re-evaluation of whether a large market is necessary to preserve the identity of this neighborhood.

There is no question that many people in Florence care deeply about San Lorenzo and want to see it flourish. Therefore, in the final analysis, this is not a story about who is right or who is wrong about San Lorenzo. Rather, it is about how a place that has been both inviting and accepting of migration, growth, change, and the unassailable right of locals and migrants to work hard and earn a living can sometimes turn mistrustful and apprehensive. That is why, in these uncertain times, what is taking place in this neighborhood and marketplace holds interest and relevance far beyond Florence.

MAP 1.1: Map of the regions of Italy, and neigboring countries

A Marketplace in Transition

Globalization is a worldwide process that draws attention from a host of academic disciplines and has given rise to new interdisciplinary fields of study. As the theorization of globalization have moved forward, scholars have identified weaknesses in approaches that fail to take cultural variability into sufficient account. Nuanced theories of globalization emphasize the importance of examining reciprocal engagements between the local and global, recognizing that diverse outcomes are possible. Steger (2013: 80), for instance, is one of many who have pointed out that given the complexity of global cultural flows, responses may vary from convergence, to new expressions of particularism, to new forms of hybridity. Of course other outcomes are possible too, including the re-empowerment of existing identities (Barth 1998; Bryceson, Okely, and Webber 2007; Comaroff and Comaroff 2009; Pellow 1996; Stacul 2003). In the best circumstances, explanations of how global flows and local variables interact on the ground are premised on the results of research methodologies that offer direct and sustained engagement with the sample population under study. To that end, this book focuses upon how one particular sample, composed mostly of outdoor vendors and their residential neighbors, is confronting and responding to globalizing processes in a marketplace in the heart of Florence. It is based on data that I collected first-hand in the course of long-term fieldwork using a research technique called participant observation, supplemented by the findings of student research assistants who worked alongside me during several of my visits to the field.

There is ample reason to describe San Lorenzo Market as a "global" marketplace. Though never ethnically homogenous, as recently as 30 years ago it was operated and frequented by a higher percentage of native-born residents than is now the case. Thus, while there were fewer vendors and shoppers in the past, proportionately more of both were Florentines. In addition to striking demographic changes, the types of items on sale in the market vary in ways that reflect greater access to foreign manufacturers and the shifting tastes and budgets of shoppers. Three decades ago, local handicrafts and textiles dominated. Today, however, vendors who sell goods that are "Made in Florence" or "Made in Italy" hasten to point out that fact to shoppers to differentiate the wares they sell from those of other merchants who do not. Local and foreign shoppers alike routinely quiz vendors regarding the provenance of their merchandise. Some even insist on knowing the provenance of the vendor. The impact of globalization is especially fascinating to consider, given that many elements of Western-style modernity, according to some scholars the precursor to globalization, originated precisely in this part of Italy. One of the interesting twists of this study, which is set in what is now a very socially diverse neighborhood, is that it probes how the "West" (or at least one Western European urban population's characteristic practices and ideas about itself) has been affected by the arrival of the "rest."

FIGURE 1.1: Aerial view of the San Lorenzo church, Central Market, and train station
CREDIT: Adobe Stock

Italy was once characterized as a country of emigration, a major exporter of labor. Large communities of the descendants of those emigrants are now found throughout the world, including in major cities such as New York, Toronto, São Paulo, Buenos Aires, and Melbourne. Today, however, much of Europe, including Italy, is a target destination "for migrations coming from Africa, Latin America, Asia and Eastern Europe" (Magatti and Quassoli 2003: 147). Some immigrants hope to settle permanently, while others regard Italy as a stop on an even longer journey. In addition to legal aliens, a significant population of undocumented immigrants resides in Italy, mostly first generation. Many find work in informal sectors, including trade and agriculture. Magatti and Quassoli (2003: 164) point out that their circumstances "favoured the diffusion of semi-dependent activities ... carried out in an informal manner, often bordering on illegality, which lacks ... long-term prospects." They note, "Once they are in the country, immigrants are easily recruited as a flexible and informal workforce ... in street selling (for years the streets in the richest cities or most popular beaches have been teeming with street vendors illegally selling all kinds of goods)" (162).

Migration of labor is one of many transnational processes associated with globalization, and global flows of people seeking to better their economic situation are a major catalyst. The history of this city reveals that Florence has participated in this process for a considerable time. European metropolitan centers were important for strengthening globalization tendencies from the start of the early modern period (Steger 2013: 29). Even before the Renaissance, Florentines engaged with peoples far beyond the Italian peninsula through commerce. In medieval times, Florentine currency was the most trusted in Europe. By the 1400s, Florentine textiles were widely exported, and some materials used in their production were imported from thousands of miles away. By the fifteenth century, Florentine bankers had established offices elsewhere on the continent, and Florentine merchants were traveling regularly to improve their business prospects (Prajda 2010).

While the culture and environment of the city have been affected by the Florentines who have ventured out of it to pursue new opportunities, so too has the city been affected by inward flows of people (Clemente 2010). Foreigners have been drawn to this dynamic entrepôt for centuries. One of San Lorenzo's main streets, via Nazionale, formerly bore the name "German Street" for the Renaissance-era textile workers who migrated there from the north and took up residence. In the nineteenth century, the *piazza* in front of the Santa Maria Novella Church just west of San Lorenzo was characterized as "The Mecca of the Foreigners," as a plaque erected there to honor the American poet Henry Wadsworth Longfellow notes. Contemporary globalization processes, including global tourism, now bring even more people and products to Florence at a staggering rate. Writers and artists from abroad continue to seek inspiration in Florence, but most visitors simply come for a great vacation. Millions arrive annually to see the sights, enjoy the cuisine, and shop. Florence continues to appear regularly at or near the top of lists of the world's most desirable vacation destinations. It should come as no surprise, therefore, that an estimated 60 per cent of businesses in Florence are linked to tourism in some way. A newspaper pointed to the centrality of tourism to the city's economy in a pithily titled article published a few years back: "Alarm! The Foreigners Aren't Invading Us" (Miller 2002: 191).

The number of international travelers to Florence grew markedly in the late 1970s and 1980s. In the course of fieldwork I spoke with many returning tourists who had been first-time visitors during those decades. Unsurprisingly, declines in the strength of major currencies, global economic downturns, and terrorism fears have serious consequences for a market in a city that relies heavily on tourism. So, too, do the choices of students pursuing study abroad. In addition to short-term tourists, students from all over the world go to Florence to study art, fashion, language, and more, like my own student research assistants did. The municipal website proclaims Florence's status as an "international city" committed to peaceful global coexistence and reciprocal comprehension.[2] Even in such a cosmopolitan setting, however, it

---

2 More information on Florence as an international city is available on the official city website. See: http://www.comune.fi.it/export/sites/retecivica/comune_firenze/relazioni_internazionali_cooperazione/introduzione.html.

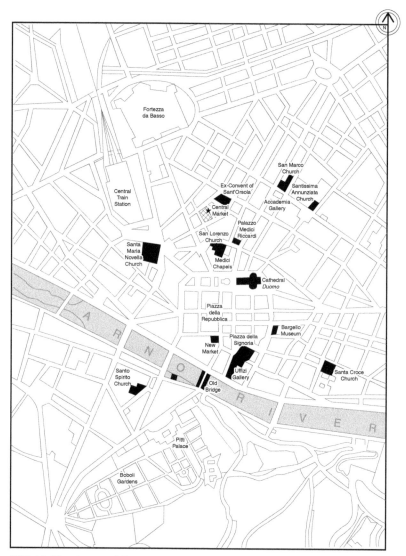

MAP 1.2: Historic center of Florence and environs

would be naïve to assume that reciprocal comprehension is an easy or natural outgrowth of globalization.

With regard to San Lorenzo, for example, one might expect that new diversity in the marketplace would simply and steadily lead to a more homogenized environment, a kind of melting-pot market. Yet as Ted Lewellen (2002: 26) cautions about the theorization of globalization generally, while there are deterministic dimensions to globalization processes, "there is nothing inevitable about the effects at the local level." Precisely how people respond to these processes is shaped by a range of variables, including "local history, culture, the physical and social environment, leadership, and individual decision making." Partly for these reasons, he claims, there is "no such thing as a passive response to globalization."

Indeed, responses to globalization processes in San Lorenzo are anything but passive. In this microsocial setting the lack of inevitability to which Lewellen points can be clearly seen in local-level responses to social change. One has been the evocation of a nostalgic desire on the part of some San Lorenzo people, or *sanlorenzini*, to return to how San Lorenzo used to be. Among long-term vendors, specifically, another response has been dismay over challenges to longstanding ways of conducting business. In San Lorenzo, where vendors work just a few feet apart, palpable tension often results from the juxtaposition of sometimes very different modes of comportment. A third response is heightened awareness of, and interest in, preserving San Lorenzo's heritage, including both its material and immaterial culture. Concerning local responses to globalization processes, then, this volume explores ideas about a quality or essence that many locals refer to as "Florentine-ness," or, more precisely, *fiorentinità*. What is implied by *fiorentinità*, how it is expressed and cultivated, is a subject of passionate debate. As this book shows, notions about *fiorentinità* vary widely, including in ways that sometimes set *sanlorenzini* themselves at odds.

San Lorenzo as a marketplace has received limited scholarly attention. But marketplaces in general have long fascinated social scientists, and some important ethnographic projects have been situated in them. One was Clifford Geertz's study of Javanese vendors, which formed part of the subject of his book *Peddlers and Princes* (1963). Geertz argued that the market shaped the whole of vendors' lives, because from their perspective it was as much a sociocultural world as a mode of economic activity. He suggested that markets were best understood by bringing three perspectives to bear: the "patterned flow of economic goods and services"; the "economic mechanisms to sustain and regulate that flow"; and the "social and cultural system in which those mechanisms are imbedded" (30).

Although praised as a landmark study (Wertheim 1964: 307), Geertz's analysis was criticized for neglecting how outside forces affected the people and the overall market system that he studied (Bruner 1966). Recent advances in globalization theory have provided tools to understand those forces better. Still, as Theodore Bestor reminds us, despite global forces swirling around them, marketplaces are indeed "demarcated" in ways that matter to our understanding of the subjectivities of those who operate within them. In the world-famous Tsukiji Fish Market where Bestor conducted fieldwork, for example, being physically present and socially connected is critical to a trader's success (Bestor 2004: 18). Notwithstanding a host of factors beyond his immediate control, including governmental regulations; local, national, and global

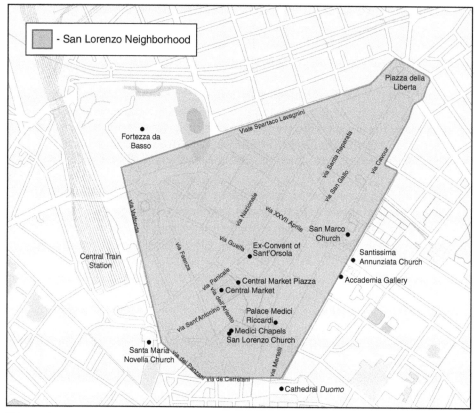

MAP 1.3: San Lorenzo neighborhood

demand for his products, and more, his social capital, or the strength and usefulness of collective networks of which he is a part, is the "bedrock" of each vendor's trade (Bestor 2004: 307). The social structure of its institutions and the cultural logic of the transactions that take place in this demarcated zone are precisely what make Tsukiji a marketplace (308).

Another scholar whose fieldwork took him to marketplaces where the local and global converge and place matters is Walter Little, who investigated the activities of Mayan handicraft vendors who sell to tourists in Antigua, Guatemala. Little's (2004: 271) research revealed that, among Kaqchikel Maya, complexes of social relationships "contribute to their subjectivities and expressed identities, including strategic and tactical forms that can rearticulate with other aspects of identity" within a transnational tourist zone. Little built upon work by other scholars of the Global South, exploring how arenas in which vending occurs serve at once to link people and differentiate or stratify them. He revealed that "Mayas incorporate themselves into the global while continuing to reinscribe significance in the local" (10) and traced not only how global forces act upon vendors, but also how vendors "conceive of, construct, maintain and use identity" in the face of them (12–13).

Our understanding of how work, local identities, and global forces intersect and influence one another has also been advanced by the studies of Florence Babb, another scholar of the Global South. She conducted fieldwork among Peruvian market women in the town of Huarez (Babb 1989). Specifically, she explored the "double burden" that her research subjects "carry as workers and as women" (204), explaining how developments in Peru's political economy have affected opportunities, life experiences, and subjectivities.

Bestor, Little, Babb, and many other scholars whose works are cited throughout this book demonstrate that marketplaces matter, as they provide rich environments in which to scrutinize the microsocial consequences of macrosocial forces. Yet the present book is not about a marketplace alone: it also addresses some broader challenges linked to social change that face a historic neighborhood in a renowned city. Carole Counihan (2004: 9–10) has suggested that "[a]nthropologists have not only ignored Florence, but they have also given relatively little attention to Italy's urban culture, a lacuna in a country with an urban tradition extending back millennia ..." The present book helps to fill that lacuna, and, in so doing, invites paired readings with some very important studies. One is Counihan's own volume on how Tuscan food practices and family life have changed over time in response to broader regional socioeconomic developments. Another study that focuses on the intersection of food and culture is Rachel Black's (2012) ethnography of Porta Palazzo, Turin's comestibles market. Three significant works set in Naples are Thomas Belmonte's (1989) ethnography of life among the poor families of "Fontana del Re," Italo Pardo's (1996) analysis of the interplay between moral and material interests in social relations among inner city residents, and Jason Pine's (2012) volume on social interactions and the search for personal opportunity within the neomelodica music scene. Another major study in a different urban setting is Michael Herzfeld's (2009) volume on the impact of gentrification on a residential population of artisans and shopkeepers in the heart of old Rome. Each of these works, in its own way, helps to direct our attention to the vast and varied Italian urban experience.

With its focus on responses to demographic and related changes, this volume contributes to understandings of Italian urban life in several ways. It offers an account of the work life and interpersonal relationships of long-term San Lorenzo vendors, providing insight into the experiences and subjectivities of *sanlorenzini* who have labored there most of their lives. It addresses how small-scale businessmen and businesswomen negotiate their professional and cultural identities in an increasingly globalized setting. And it explores how ideas about *fiorentinità* are implicated in efforts to preserve and reinvigorate this neighborhood, or, as many put it, to "Save San Lorenzo."

Like the Japanese fish merchants Bestor interviewed half a world away in Tsukiji, and the displaced artisans and shopkeepers Herzfeld befriended in Rome, *sanlorenzini* also occupy a space that they consider "a repository of cultural heritage" (Bestor 2004: 19). To a large degree, many in San Lorenzo regard themselves as guardians of tradition. That role must be taken into consideration when examining their responses to migration, how they deal with civic officials, and how they answer the question of whether *fiorentinità* can or even should be restored to this neighborhood.

Migrations and Complications

At first glance, the San Lorenzo Market seems confusing. It meanders across a broad swath of streets and three *piazze*. First-time visitors often conclude that its geography is fluid and that vendors simply set up wherever they find a spot. Official demarcations are clearly identifiable, however, once carts are removed. Appurtenant streets and squares are stenciled with thick white lines that delineate vendors' allotted spaces: each numbered block represents a space for one business. The official starting point, space number one, was located in the church square (Piazza San Lorenzo) across from the Medici Palace.[3] The area around the church was always considered a pre-eminent location because it is closest to Florence's cathedral and heavily trafficked by tourists. Just recently, however, outdoor vendors were removed from the piazza and told that they could no longer work there. Many vendors indicated their resistance to the move with demonstrations and petitions to the city's leaders, as later chapters show. A second prime area has always been Silver Street, where I spend most of my time, and where the front entrance to the Central Market building is located.

Regardless of the street or piazza on which they find themselves, many who labor there are very proud of their association with this neighborhood. In fact, images of beaming local entrepreneurs posed in shops and market stands were focal points of a 2008 photographic exhibit co-sponsored by the Marangoni photographic gallery and a neighborhood organization, "Together for San Lorenzo." Entitled "San Lorenzo: A Neighborhood on the Move," the exhibit was San Lorenzo's first foray into one of the city's annual initiatives, "the Florentine Genius Project" (Filardo and Savorelli 2008). Sponsored by the provincial government, the initiative invites Tuscans to rediscover their history and "become conscious of their potential and their role in society." It was no coincidence that each merchant whose photograph appeared in San Lorenzo's entry held a card or poster bearing a handwritten appeal to the government for

---

3 The Palazzo Medici Riccardi, originally the Palazzo Medici, is located at via Cavour 1. For more on its history, see the official website at: http://www.palazzo-medici.it.

FIGURE 1.2: Silver Street vendor's *banco* open for business
CREDIT: Anne Schiller

more neighborhood improvements. Nor was it coincidence that immigrant entrepreneurs were featured along with *sanlorenzini* born in the neighborhood. Diversity was highlighted as a positive feature of neighborhood life.

As the exhibit title suggested, San Lorenzo is indeed on the move. Or at least it is a place of comings and goings. A significant number of Florentines have moved elsewhere, although some new ones have relocated there. Aspiring entrepreneurs from many parts of the world have opened businesses. Some live in the neighborhood, although many commute each day. One challenge facing the neighborhood, however, is that it has become a magnet for undocumented immigrants. Included in that category are *abusivi*, or "infringers," irregular vendors who attempt to sell merchandise on the fly while staying a step ahead of police patrols. Not all infringers are irregular immigrants, however. Some are documented immigrants who simply do not hold a vending license. Every morning, infringers can be seen disembarking from trains and trams at the Santa Maria Novella Station laden with enormous bags of merchandise. They head out from the station to the San Lorenzo market or other heavily touristed parts of the city. Competition with so-called infringers, who do not pay taxes or fees for the use of public space, is a source of exasperation and frustration for many licensed vendors. Shouting matches and scuffles between irregular vendors and the police, and between legal and illegal vendors, have erupted repeatedly and are widely covered by the press. Headlines that have appeared in recent years concerning these episodes include: "Revolt in San Lorenzo. The Neighborhood Descends to the Streets. Tension with the Infringers" (Plastina 2005); "Invasion of Infringers" (*La Nazione* 2006); "Far West in San Lorenzo. It Is War in the Market. Ambulant Vendors and Infringers, Coexistence Impossible" (Agostini 2007); "San Lorenzo in the Hands of Infringers. Canadian Tourist Hurt, The Merchants: There Are Controls But They Are More Aggressive" (*La Nazione* 2008), "Fines Only for Ambulant Vendors. It Is Revolt Against Infringers" (Baldi 2009); "San Lorenzo, Here We Go Again: Infringers Assault Tourists" (*Il Firenze* 2009); and "Shoves and Threats, One Step from a Brawl, Merchants and [Infringers] at Short Swords" (Gianni 2013). Dozens of similar articles could also be cited that report on unpleasant or violent episodes.[4]

My own introduction to the challenges and anxieties in this neighborhood was rather dramatic, occurring at the very start of my fieldwork. I had become intrigued by the marketplace as a potential research site in the course of taking language lessons at a private institute located a block away from the Central Market building. A family of merchants agreed to take me on as a retail volunteer, and I embraced that opportunity to begin a qualitative study of vendors' experiences in a market that so frequently found itself on the front pages of newspapers.

As I headed to my field site on day two of my sales apprenticeship, a pair of hand-lettered posters affixed to the doors of Saint Joseph's Oratory caught my eye. Saint Joseph's, a tiny chapel patronized mostly by the elderly on their way to market, is situated on Saint Antonino Street, one of many that feed into the outdoor market area. I occasionally stopped inside to enjoy this contemplative space and was surprised to find the doors locked. I read the posters but could not entirely grasp their intent. I took notes and decided to come back with a camera. The next morning I found three posters, rather than two, attached to the oratory doors. While I was photographing those doors, more posters were being surreptitiously plastered elsewhere by unseen residents and shopkeepers. Within the hour, dozens had been fastened to the sides of buildings, secured to light poles, and taped to shop windows. Among the messages:

The institutions have	We are Abusive	San Lorenzo
left us to the delinquents	to Remove	Dirty Streets
	Abuse	Degraded Bivouacs
		Abusive Illegality
		The Shame
		of Florence

---

4 In a tragic and unusual incident in December 2011, a self-described ultra-nationalist shot and killed two immigrant vendors from Senegal and wounded three others before committing suicide in the Central Market's parking garage. For an English-language article on the attack see: http://www.florencedailynews.com/2011/12/13/double-murder-at-the-market/.

And on Saint Joseph's firmly bolted entrance:

Don't Touch Lina   Lina is All of Us   We Want More Security

I sprinted up and down Saint Antonino Street, scribbling and taking pictures. A short distance ahead, a group was gathering at the intersection where Saint Antonino Street opens on the outdoor marketplace. Some urged onlookers to join them, while others frantically shouted into cellphones: "We are at the intersection of Saint Antonino and Silver Street. Come now! Hurry!" Demonstrators blocked the intersection with large cardboard boxes identical to ones on which some illegal vendors display their wares. Many participants pinned sheets of paper to their chests that read, "Enough Criminality, We Want Security." Though spontaneous and short-lived, the protest drew local television crews, newspaper reporters, City Council members and other politicians, trade union representatives, and staff from various social-welfare organizations. Within two hours the interviews were over, the boxes had disappeared, and the crowd of about 70 had dispersed.

That flash mob in May 2005 acquainted me with concerns about social change and other issues in San Lorenzo that I continue to follow. "Lina," whose name was blazoned on the posters affixed to the oratory doors, was an elderly church caretaker attacked by two non-Italian men. Upon their arrest it was determined that one was in Italy illegally. In hopes of stealing the offertory, they had hidden inside a confessional. When Lina discovered them, they beat her. The attack left her with broken ribs and missing teeth. I learned that this was not the first time vendors and residents had jammed the streets to bring attention to what they describe as "decay." Several groups held marches. A decade later, rallies continue to be planned. Even now, when no one is looking, anonymous posters addressing these same types of issues are affixed to the sides of buildings up and down these streets.

Many *sanlorenzini*, and others, too, share the premise that more should be done to address the zone's problems. At public demonstrations the specific problem addressed and the remedy promoted for it typically reflect the organizer's point of view. What made "Lina's" protest different from others, according to participants at the time, was that it was "spontaneous." No single person, committee, or political party had organized it. Several assured me that they were drawn to the streets at that moment simply because they were "emotional." "I am really fed up," shouted a woman carrying a poster that read, in English, "HAS ANYONE SEEN THE POLICE?" "This is our market, and this is our neighborhood. If people like me keep moving away, it won't be ours anymore. We are here to save San Lorenzo," she said.

"Saving San Lorenzo" is a call to action among many. Yet while the marketplace is an important site of commerce, the motivations of those who seek to act on its behalf can be only partly explained in economic terms. The fate

FIGURE 1.3: Merchant and residents protest neighborhood crime. Sign reads, "We work well every day with foreigners. But we work very badly with drug dealers, thieves, gypsies, and infringers."
CREDIT: Anne Schiller

of San Lorenzo also evokes strong reactions because of its association with loss of heritage. During that demonstration in 2005, for example, I heard the market variously described as a repository of "heritage," of "identity," and of *fiorentinità*. Demonstrators told me that its physical deterioration (at that time plastic bottles clogged storm drains, broken glass littered the street, and there was a pungent odor of urine in adjacent streets) betokened a loss of *fiorentinità*. Although many necessary and handsome repairs have

FIGURE 1.4: Resident wearing placard that reads "Enough with criminality, we want security."
CREDIT: Anne Schiller

since been funded by the city government and private sources, including the renovation and reinvention of the market building's first floor as a venue for wine bars, restaurants, pubs, and a cooking school, one continues to hear references to the relative absence or presence of *fiorentinità*.[5]

5   The original call for expressions of interest in space on the market building's first floor is available at: http://www.comune.fi.it/opencms/export/sites/retecivica/materiali/bandi_patrimonio/avvisi/avviso_Mercato_San_Lorenzo.pdf. For more information on some businesses and activities in the Central Market today, see https//it-it.facebook.com/ilmercatocentrale.

As my fieldwork moved forward and I gained more of an insider's perspective, I became interested in how ideas about qualities associated with *fiorentinità* figured in the construction of identities as well as notions regarding heritage preservation. While the focus of my study was a host population, undergoing "intense and unavoidable" contact with alien groups (De Vos and Romanucci-Ross 2006: 380), my work benefited greatly from hearing non-Florentine stakeholders' views. Without a doubt, my multidimensional strategy of observing interactions among vendors and between vendors and customers, living in the neighborhood, and working as an unpaid sales assistant in San Lorenzo deepened my understanding of the complex relationships among culture, identities, social change, and globalization in this marketplace. It also helped me, following Lyon and Wells, to better understand the extent to which tourists as well as local stakeholders figure in the shaping and presentation of cultural heritage (Lyon and Wells 2012).

For as much as it is a place to shop, then, the San Lorenzo Market is also a dynamic field of interpersonal interaction distinguished by high levels of social diversity. It is an ephemeral space crisscrossed almost every moment by vendors and customers from around the globe who engage each other year round. Under ordinary circumstances, "the definitions of the [interactual] situation projected by the several different participants are sufficiently attuned to one another so that open contradiction will not occur" (Goffman 1959: 9). Circumstances in San Lorenzo today, however, are extraordinary. Differences in opinion occur openly regarding how one should comport oneself there and how this contested space should be managed. Consensus among merchants, customers, residents, and local officials remains elusive. My goal has been to probe the complexities and ambiguities that characterize this neighborhood in order to gain insight into some identities and traditions at play—and at work—in San Lorenzo today.

Civic Administration and Politics in San Lorenzo

To be clear, "Florence" refers to two distinct but overlapping jurisdictional entities. The first, the Province of Florence, is a province (similar to a county) within the Region of Tuscany. It is headed by a president. The second, the City of Florence, is the capital of the Tuscan region, and governed by a mayor. Earlier I suggested that San Lorenzo's story begins at the doors of its church, but the venue that figures just as prominently in more recent installments is Florence's town hall, the Palazzo Vecchio. The Palazzo Vecchio houses the Office of the Mayor and is the seat of meetings of the City Council, an administrative-political body that confers with the mayor. Recommendations of the City Council, decisions by the mayor, and projects led by officials who comprise the 10-member Mayor's Cabinet affect nearly all dimensions of public life and infrastructure. That fact is very clear in San Lorenzo, where the state of things is frequently the subject of council deliberation and fodder for government press conferences. A brief introduction to the city's administrative organization and the broad outline of local politics is a useful prologue for later understanding of what is, at times, a prickly relationship between some *sanlorenzini* and Florence's elected leadership.

Like Bologna, its northern neighbor, and some other important cities in the Region of Tuscany, Florence is generally associated with left-leaning politics, although a broad spectrum of parties operates there. The City Council includes representatives of majority and minority political parties. Seats are filled through a combination of popular election, proportional election, and appointment. Proportional apportionment secures representation for smaller factions. Candidates who place second through fifth in mayoral elections win council seats. The mayor fills other seats by appointment.

The process of choosing a mayor of Florence has changed over time. The selection of a mayor today is based on direct vote, but this has been the case only since fairly recently. From Italian unification until 1926, the city's highest official was handpicked by the leading noble of the region, usually a duke. After the Fascist Party came to power and until it was deposed in 1945, the Fascist government appointed Florence's mayor. Between 1945 and 1995, the City Council chose the mayor. Residents have elected their mayor since 1995 in mayoral elections that are held every five years.[6]

Given the large number of parties and the modest number of council seats, the significance of coalitions to the outcome of political races is enormous. National and local coalitions are constantly in flux, as factions form within larger groups which then affect coalitions' ideological centers. For example, the Italian socialist and communist factions have changed their names and guiding principles several times in the past 20 years, joining and then leaving the left-wing coalition *L'Ulivo* (literally "The Olive Tree"). *L'Ulivo* itself changed so much over its tenure that it dissolved in 2007, with the bulk of its members moving to the new *Partito Democratico* (literally

---

6 To accommodate all the candidates, the election process has an option of two rounds: a general election that includes every candidate, and a run-off election between the top two first-round finishers, if necessary. If a candidate achieves more than half of the general vote in the first round, as in 1995 and 1999, then no second round is required. The second round, if necessary, is a run-off election held two to three weeks later. The top two first-round candidates are the ones on the ballot, and they must garner support from defeated candidates' factions. In 2004 and 2009 the winning candidate garnered over 60 per cent of the vote through the shifting allegiances of the two-round system. Many parties are small, and despite their popularity in their electoral district, they lack a sufficiently large base to affect local or provincial politics, let alone regional or national politics. Therefore, political parties form coalitions in support of a candidate. The flexible nature of coalitions is partly a result of the multi-round election system, where factions shift their allegiance to a second-round candidate if their first-round candidate is defeated.

"Democratic Party") of Matteo Renzi. Renzi served as president of the province of Florence from 2004 to 2009, mayor of the city of Florence from 2009 to 2014, and went on to become Italy's fifty-sixth prime minister. His successor as mayor of Florence was Dario Nardella, also from the Democratic Party. Right-leaning coalitions exhibit similar adjustments to their voting blocs, but their situation is compounded by their weaker presence in Florence. Despite former prime minister Silvio Berlusconi's success at the national level, for instance, his conservative party, *Forza Italia* (literally "Go Italy," with reference to the sport chant), was never able to win a major election in Florence.

While Florence's elected leadership is consistently composed of representatives of the liberal party, the views of conservative candidates are closer to those of many San Lorenzo vendors, at least anecdotally.[7] In my experience, right-leaning candidates hold better-attended events in San Lorenzo than do left-leaning candidates. Merchants I know best suggest a variety of reasons for their preference. These include perceptions that the left is soft on immigration, is prone to hiking taxes on business, and, in particular among outdoor vendors, increases burdens on legal vendors while doing little to prevent illegal vending.

Unlicensed vendors originate from many countries. Those from Africa are sometimes referred to by the idiom "*Vu Comprà*" or "You Want to Buy," reflecting their imperfect grasp of Italian, facility in French, and what they are most often heard calling out to passersby. That particular idiom, which has very negative connotations, seems to be used less than in the past. Registered ambulant merchants and others mostly deploy the term "infringers" to identify unlicensed vendors. Infringers display goods on the tops of cardboard boxes, on sheets spread out on the street, or in display cases that can be quickly shut if they need to disguise what they are doing. Some fasten merchandise to the inside of umbrellas that can be snapped opened or closed in seconds. Some display pictures of their wares on cell phone screens to passersby to avoid having to carry stock around and risk its confiscation. Dozens of infringers can be seen operating in San Lorenzo on nearly any given day, displaying goods on the steps of the Central Market building, in the intersections of marketplace pedestrian walkways, or on the sidewalk next to the doorways of shops. In the course of many afternoons my student research assistants and I have counted upwards of 50 irregular vendors plying wares in these locations, some individuals vanishing and reappearing as the hours, or the police, pass by.

In an effort to ameliorate problems that affect life in this zone, *san-lorenzini* remain in constant dialogue with civic officials, yet not all *san-lorenzini* agree on what steps those authorities should pursue. In December 2013, for example, the mayor authorized the removal of dozens of licensed

---

7 The market vendors' apparent political conservatism puts them in the minority. Each of Florence's three elected mayors has been politically left of center, although right-leaning coalitions and parties maintain a visible presence. The proportional voting system provides the latter with a voice in the City Council.

ambulant vendors from the San Lorenzo Church piazza. That decision was portrayed as part of a larger program to restore *fiorentinità*. Its implementation evoked widespread protests and strikes among some *sanlorenzini* and jubilation among others. To understand why reactions vary, one must know more about living and working in San Lorenzo, which the techniques of qualitative research enable us to learn.

Fieldwork as an Apprentice Vendor

Previous sections introduced some of the ways in which *sanlorenzini* have responded to changes in their environment. Positioning myself to ask and answer questions about change in San Lorenzo required me to make a considerable shift in geographic focus and to enlarge my linguistic toolkit. I had studied Italian as an undergraduate anthropology major and even considered conducting dissertation research in Italy. But graduate studies led me down a different path. I became a specialist in Southeast Asia and learned to speak Indonesian. For two decades, the subject of my scholarly research and writing was indigenous activism in the rainforests of Indonesian Borneo, or Kalimantan. In Kalimantan I lived among horticultural peoples who inhabited remote villages without electricity or running water. My fieldwork activities on any given day might have included helping neighbors harvest rice, fishing with friends at the river's edge, taking notes at a sacrifice in honor of the village guardian, or teaching English to youngsters who in turn helped me to improve my command of the local language, Ngaju Dayak.

Directly engaging in the daily activities of one's research subjects, as I did in Kalimantan, is basic to a type of qualitative research methodology called participant observation.[8] DeWalt and DeWalt (2011: 5) have characterized participant observation as a methodology that involves living in the research context over an extended period, learning and using the local language, actively participating in a wide range of regular and extraordinary activities with people who are full participants in the setting, using everyday conversation as an interview technique, observing informally during one's free time, recording observations, and using tacit and explicit information in analysis and writing. Some researchers refer to participant observation as an "apprenticeship" that leads to new perspectives and "intensive enculturation" (11). Wax (1971: 363) noted that fieldwork of this type is itself "as much a

---

8 Participant observation enables researchers to collect data in relatively "natural" settings, in contrast to formal interviews and experiments arranged specifically for research purposes. The researcher must first "find some role in the field being studied, and this will usually have to be done at least through implicit, and probably also through explicit, negotiation with people in that field …. access cannot be assumed to be available automatically, relations will have to be established, and identities co-constructed" through negotiations and renegotiations with the subjects being studied (Hammersley and Atkinson 2007: 4).

social phenomenon (involving reciprocity, complex role-playing, the invention and obeying of rules, mutual assistance, and play) as it is an individual phenomenon … good fieldwork is not something performed by an isolated intellectual or researcher but something created by all of the people in the social situation being studied." Participant observation is a very demanding methodology, but it is unparalleled for enabling researchers to achieve a deep understanding of the perspectives of members of the population under study. As it is characterized by an emergent research strategy, and because interviews are usually open-ended, participant observation often leads to unexpected insights, as it certainly has in my own work.

While I was conducting research and publishing about Indonesia, I retained a personal interest in learning Italian. Indeed, at one point while I lived in Kalimantan, I continued my language study with an Italian priest who had been posted to a town in the eastern part of the island. When the opportunity presented itself, I signed up for Italian classes at the university where I taught in the United States, as well as adult education courses in conversational Italian. I supplemented those efforts with summer language study in Florence, credited as the birthplace of modern Italian. From 1999 to 2005, I visited Florence annually for language training. I also served as resident director of a study-abroad program based at the Lorenzo de' Medici Institute for 10 summers beginning in 1999. Exploring the market with my students and hearing how much they enjoyed shopping there piqued my interest in the marketplace as a site of cross-cultural encounter. Listening to vendors and residents chat informally about their lives and livelihoods as I drank *espresso* at a local bar between my Italian classes ultimately inspired me to launch a research project there. This book is based on the results of anthropological fieldwork that officially began in 2005 and which I continue to pursue during annual trips to the field, most recently in 2015.

The geographical and physical settings of this and my prior projects are vastly different, yet the work itself has important common threads. One is methodological: both utilize intensive, long-term participant observation. Another is theoretical: both focus on how individuals and groups construct and express identity when confronted with dramatic social and economic changes brought by globalization. For example, my informants and friends in Kalimantan were coping with the consequences of government policy regarding transmigration, whereby individuals from other ethnic groups with very different languages, religions, and cultures were resettled and given title to agricultural lands that local people claimed by right of customary law. Furthermore, multinational logging and mining operations had damaged the environment to the extent that these people were less able to depend upon forests and rivers as sources of food or products that they could trade or sell for cash. Many responded by engaging in identity politics and cultivating allegiances based on their traditional religion, or on pan-Dayak or global indigeneity (Schiller 1997; 2001; 2007).

In Florence, I encountered a situation where issues of identity also weighed heavily. Over the past three decades, large numbers of immigrants, including asylum seekers, have arrived in Italy. Permanent immigration to Italy remains at high levels, and the registered foreign population is now over eight per cent.[9] More than five million registered foreign immigrants live in Italy today. Undocumented migration to Italy and to the Mediterranean region continues to attract much attention in the world press, including coverage of tragic losses of life when those attempting to enter Europe by boat do not succeed in reaching shore. In 2014, more than 170,000 asylum seekers and refugees arrived in Italy by sea. By the end of the third quarter of 2015, an additional 130,000 had managed to survive the crossing.

Political unrest in North Africa and the Middle East has contributed to a spike in migration inflows, and Italy is among the countries on the "front lines" of what has been called an "unprecedented humanitarian crisis" of "unparalled numbers" (Organisation for Economic Co-operation and Development 2015). In Italy, as in other industrialized democracies, the phenomenon of immigration is associated with both challenges and opportunities. Competing interests lead in many cases to policy paralysis, which encourages those who are willing to shoulder the risks that immigration may require (Hollifield, Martin, and Orrenius 2014: 4). In the service sector, for example, the availability of low-wage migrant workers may offer short-term benefits to some employers and address problems of labor shortages. Depending upon whether migrants are eligible for housing and other social benefits, the larger national costs of immigration may be immediate or deferred. The consequences of immigration extend far beyond their impact on an economy, however. The presence of immigrants, legal or other, may have direct repercussions for and on the culture of a host society, as this book shows.[10]

---

9 For more information on immigration rates in Italy, see www.istat.it.

10 While immigration is a global issue of major importance, the manner in which states respond to it is shaped by national history, geography, cultural attitudes, economic and political exigencies, and other factors. Terrorist incidents and fear of global terrorism also increasingly have an influence in this regard. Canada and the United States, for example, both have robust traditions of immigration yet have responded differently on issues of political asylum (García y Griego 1992). States also vary in the extent to which they may be compelled to take the political actions of neighboring nations into account. It is instructive to consider, for instance, how protection of internal borders, labor markets, and external borders has been affected by the creation of the European Single Market which, as Brochmann (1996: 4) has noted, "involves subtle mechanisms which are hard to trace empirically, but which might nevertheless have a bearing on attitudes towards foreigners." Differences in border-control practices also shed light on relations among nations, as strategies range from open borders, to controlled borders maintained with maritime or aerial surveillance or physical or virtual fences, to "sealed" borders. For a useful discussion of border control practices with particular reference to North American and Europe, see Vallet (2014).

In Florence, a city of nearly 400,000, registered foreign immigrants comprise nearly seven per cent of the population. While attention is directed at identifying irregular immigrants as well, that population is fluid and there is no agreement about their number (Bonanni 2013). The fact that many migrants, registered and unregistered, seek commercial-sector employment is apparent to nearly everyone who visits, including tourists. In San Lorenzo, where many immigrants earn their living, certain streets are associated with immigrants from particular countries, such as "Chinatown," "Little Manila," and so on. In addition to retail work, some immigrants are employed as porters or as members of set-up and break-down crews. A question I often hear debated is whether San Lorenzo is a Florentine, Italian, or multicultural market. In that regard, as was my experience in Kalimantan, many "natives" claim that their ability to earn a living or to preserve local culture has been compromised by some incomers. It was clear to me early on that in Florence, as in Kalimantan, globalization evokes passionate discussions about relationships between local culture and identity.

By 2005, my Italian had reached the point where people could easily converse with me, a criterion critical to becoming a full participant observer. I expressed interest to close friends in apprenticing with a vendor, and one of them made a match. A family of Florentine merchants who have operated a business on Silver Street for generations offered me a chance, and I began working as their volunteer. I have continued to volunteer for the Beati-Blandae family ever since. I consider them my principal workplace mentors and, now, personal friends. Members of this hardworking family are introduced in more detail in Chapter Three. Over the years I have also established relationships with other merchants across the marketplace. Through my own efforts, those of the Beati-Blandae family, and through other friends, my network of contacts continues to grow.

To date I have logged over 1,000 hours in direct sales of artisanal handwork. I have passed hundreds more conducting observations. I have carried out formal interviews with a cross-section of stakeholders, cross-checked my data with informants, attended community meetings and events, and consulted a host of archival sources. As a sales assistant I enjoy opportunities to interact with shoppers from across the globe. I often interview them about their experiences in San Lorenzo, and I report on some of those findings in this book. I also involved eight undergraduate students as field research assistants over the decade that I served as visiting resident director of a study-abroad program on which my university collaborated with the Lorenzo de'Medici Institute. Some were anthropology majors, but others were from design, psychology, and biochemistry. None of the students spoke Italian, but they brought many other skills. Each collaborated with me to design original field projects that complemented larger research goals. Some worked as volunteer sales staff in the outdoor market, Central

Market building, or nearby shops. Merchants were impressed by their commitment and appreciated the hands-on assistance. Others were charged with conducting surveys directed at English-speaking shoppers regarding their impressions of the market and its history. Some others made maps or were tasked with documenting vendors' and shoppers' behavior on observation protocol sheets. Dozens of students not directly involved in the research shared photographs or stories about their experiences. The project has thus benefited enormously from the contributions of undergraduate researchers. These talented students also came away with stronger research skills to draw upon in their future careers.

My time investment notwithstanding, I remain an outsider not completely absorbed in the marketplace scene. Whenever I meet people connected with San Lorenzo, I consider it my ethical responsibility to identify myself as an anthropologist who is conducting research in addition to being a sales assistant, a practice that can interject social distance. Before engaging in any interview I ask permission to jot down informants' comments, noting that I will record them under a pseudonym and could potentially use them later in publications. Still, although my research may be considered unusual, my presence is not. Many non-Italians work in San Lorenzo, including the occasional American. If not a full participant, I am at least a recognized and expected fixture for part of each year. Vendors often consult me about language, converse with me about the latest news, or introduce me to clients or friends. I am asked to keep an eye on enterprises and to greet and try to retain potential customers while vendors step away. We chat over coffee in Silver Street's popular H13 Bar, operated by Pasqualino and Assunta, who relocated to Florence from Puglia. Vendors invite me for meals and some weekend social activities. I have also cultivated relationships in the broader neighborhood. I live in San Lorenzo most summers, frequent local businesses, and attend events hosted by the neighborhood association and other committees and groups whenever I can. Although many people on Silver Street recognize me, I have made an effort to keep them from being recognized in turn. Almost every individual in this book has been given a pseudonym. Most of them were chosen by my informants themselves, some of whom I invited to comment on the manuscript for this book before publication.

As mentioned previously, the majority of those whose experiences and perspectives are captured in this study are Florentines by birth, although my sample also includes some other ethnic Italians or naturalized citizens who have passed most of their working lives in this city. While I have interviewed dozens of vendors and perhaps three dozen residents at length in the course of this project, and had numerous occasions to interact with civic leaders and noted political figures in Florence, I estimate that my group of key informants numbers about 40. Three-quarters are Italian-born, and more than half are from Florence. That most of my key informants are Florentine is wholly intentional: it would not have been possible to build relationships of trust with those merchants if I had been observed devoting equal time in conversation with new arrivals, in particular irregular vendors who do not possess vending licenses. Why that activity would have compromised relations with my key informants becomes readily apparent in subsequent chapters. Also, if my target population had been non-Italians, I would certainly have devoted my precious hours of study to learning a different language in which to conduct interviews.

To understand whose voices are heard in this study, then, it is important to be familiar with some taxonomic distinctions that figure in how *sanlorenzini* talk about social difference. One has to do with who is Florentine. While native-born Florentines are Italian citizens, there are many people in Florence who became Italian citizens through naturalization. As they are Italians who are residents of Florence, they sometimes refer to themselves as Florentines, although few *sanlorenzini* born there would consider them to be so. Another distinction has to do with legal versus illegal vendors, both of whom operate openly in this neighborhood. Immigrants with legal vending permits can be considered *sanlorenzini*, because of the location of their work life, but no one I know would consider them Florentines. Most illegal vendors are not ethnically Italians, although there is certainly a handful of Italians, including a few *sanlorenzini*, who engage in unlicensed petty trade. Beyond ethnicity, a critical difference between those irregulars and the other illegal vendors discussed in this book is that Italian petty vendors do not set up displays of merchandise to compete openly with legal vendors. Rather, they sell items from discreet satchels or small over-the-shoulder bags. There are also some legal immigrants to Italy who do not have vending permits but do work illegally in San Lorenzo as vendors. To my knowledge, I was never personally mistaken for an illegal worker, as it was widely known that my activities were unremunerated.

Again, this study's subject population consists mostly of *sanlorenzini* of Florentine parentage. Key informants also include some other long-term vendors, Italian by birth, who migrated to Florence many years ago. I have worked among and developed friendships with some naturalized Italian citizens in San Lorenzo as well, primarily Persians who have worked in the market for decades. I count three of them as key informants and good friends. One can easily take the broad view and say there are many kinds of Florentines. This book is dedicated to all of them, but it does not take all of them as its subject.

Given demographics and in view of the special place that San Lorenzo occupies in the public consciousness, I am often cautioned as I do fieldwork that I have arrived 30 years too late to conduct an ethnographic study there of a Florentine market, because few Florentines remain. I am sometimes told that I should transfer my project to the Saint Ambrogio Market near Santa

Croce Church, as I may find more Florentines across town.[11] In distinction to those who would argue that San Lorenzo's moment has passed, however, I find its diversity to be a powerful part of its anthropological allure. In fact, this marketplace and neighborhood offer an ideal setting in which to investigate some consequences of global–local interaction on identities in a venue that is, at one and the same time, exquisitely unique and manifestly ordinary.

Marketplace Performance in the Theater of Sales

Some readers of this study are likely to have visited San Lorenzo. If you went there on a busy day, you may have been part of a throng of shoppers standing shoulder to shoulder, inching its way along marketplace streets or through the aisles in the indoor market building. Perhaps you sampled balsamic vinegars or came face to face with some of the market's more eccentric personalities. Poldo is a stout fellow whose looks many vendors compare affectionately to those of Gabibbo, the bouncy, fleecy, enormous red blob with feet and a bib that appears on the popular satirical evening television program "The News Slithers." For 10 months of the year, Poldo purchases and packages lottery tickets in envelopes inscribed "ENVELOPE OF FORTUNE," which he sells to a compassionate vendor clientele that helps him make ends meet. As he can, he sells them an occasional broken key chain or damaged plush animal, too. Vendors who know him best recognize that he has some special needs and accord him special kindness. Some give him a euro or two toward a meal; the most generous wash his laundry. In July and August, Poldo travels west to the island of Elba to sell doughnuts on the beach. By late May, Poldo may already be sporting his "Donut Man" tee-shirt as he makes his usual marketplace rounds. The "Florentine Elvis," actually born in Naples, is another fixture. His ducktail updo and colorful costumes win him frequent requests for photographs, which he hopes will bring him tips. Once every few years he reportedly manages to visit Elvis's mansion, Graceland, on those earnings. Also, "Mister Violet," whose violet hair, violet pants, soccer team shirt, and violet face paint make him among the most identifiable of the Fiorentina team's fans, is frequently found there chatting with friends on days when a soccer match is scheduled. On Silver Street, where I work, there are also some much more understated but equally well-known characters for whom we remain on the lookout. One is George the bread man, usually wearing an apron and short pants covered in flour, who dashes up and down the street delivering orders from his business inside the Central Market building. Another is Jacopo, the fruit and vegetable

---

11 The Saint Ambrogio Market has also been a subject of anthropological inquiry. See Lelli
    (2010). Concerning socioeconomic change in another market in Tuscany, see Valente (2003).

FIGURE 1.5: An olive oil, vinegar, cheese, and preserved meats merchant inside the Central Market building.
CREDIT: Christina Gordon

vendor, who rarely stops by for a chat without bringing a bunch of grapes or a container of cherries for everyone he visits to enjoy.

For most foreign visitors, San Lorenzo epitomizes an "Italian market." For *sanlorenzini* and others in Florence, the identity of this marketplace is much more ambiguous. As already pointed out, they often raise the question of whether this marketplace is Florentine, Italian, or multicultural. They have certain indicators in mind when they do so. For example, in the opening of

FIGURE 1.6: Silver Street aerial scene with the cathedral bell tower in the distance (1980s).
CREDIT: Antonio Lelli

this chapter I referred to a leaflet I once saw that characterized San Lorenzo as a "symphony of racket." Yet while I personally find the marketplace to be quite noisy, many Florentines lament that it has become disturbingly quiet.

Fieldwork has enabled me to understand that this perception is linked to a decline in the usage of the local dialect, *fiorentino*. For some, the absence of *fiorentino* is evidence that the market is no longer Florentine. But language is not the sole indicator. Another has to do with comportment—of vendors as well as of shoppers.

As becomes clear in subsequent chapters, the present study foregrounds what I call "marketplace performance," which I define as the way in which merchants comport themselves in interactions with clients, fellow vendors, and other people central to earning a living there. The focus is thus quite different from what economists would term "market performance," or the extent to which a business or industry meets particular objectives including production, employment, and distribution targets. During my studies I found that San Lorenzo vendors easily objectify many aspects of their marketplace performances. I was not long into fieldwork, in fact, when a member of the family that owns the business where I volunteer made a remark that demonstrated it. A Protestant missionary from the United States stopped to examine the merchandise. After some casual conversation about our unusual circumstances, an American professor trying to sell merchandise to an American missionary on behalf of a Florentine vendor, the owner commented concerning my nascent sales technique: "She's a born *imbonitrice*." My initial reaction was to blanch. Two possible translations of the word *imbonitrice*, specifically "huckster" and "fast talker," are tinged with disrepute. A third choice, however, is "show woman." Given the vendor's personal history, coupled with the highly self-reflexive nature of the remark with respect to his own livelihood, I suggest that performance and showmanship in the theater of sales were foremost in his mind.

Over the course of fieldwork, I became acquainted with various rules that govern marketplace performances. Although vending is a "natural" talent according to many of my informants, it is very much a cultural act and learned behavior. Through observation, conversation, and outright instruction from more experienced marketers, I learned to interact with customers in a manner considered appropriate by my mentors' standards. I also observed that not all vendors comported with clients in that way. Those differences are scrutinized, exteriorized, and sometimes criticized by my key informants as being incongruent with *fiorentinità*. Thus I became aware that one response to globalization in San Lorenzo has been the objectification of *fiorentinità* as a dimension of marketplace performance and part of professional identity. But vending was not the only arena in which *fiorentinità* was discussed. I also noted the deployment of the concept to very different ends in exchanges about who or what belongs in this marketplace, as later chapters show.

How identities are constructed and operationalized, and how relationships among identities that can be called personal, cultural, ethnic, national, or other, are questions of interest to scholars in many fields. Stryker, Owens, and White (2000: 6) describe the ambiguity of relations between personal and collective identities as the consequence of a "failure to ask questions" about how these "may (or may not) fit together." Some important contributions to understanding the interface are currently being made by researchers interested in social movements, including those with a particular interest in why and when subjects invoke one identity rather than another (Stryker, Owens, and White 2000: 34). These contemporary researchers build upon the contributions of earlier theorists and ethnographers.

Concerning how identities are performed in public settings, for example, Erving Goffman made a distinction long ago between information that one "gives" and information that he or she "gives off" (Goffman 1959: 2). The former refers to communication in the traditional sense of what we say, the latter to more theatrical, contextual, and non-verbal communication (4), including much of what I call marketplace performance. Meyrowitz (1990: 68) suggests that "social roles are literally performances that must ... to some extent, consciously or unconsciously, be planned and rehearsed." As we interact with audiences, "the impressions of ourselves that we foster ... act like 'promissory notes' that convey a commitment on our part to behave in the same way in the future" (68). That consistency across time and interactions, which Goffman elsewhere called "ground rules" (1971: x), is what Geertz referred to in a different context as the "etiquette of marketplace contact" (1978: 31).

Regarding social performances, Goffman distinguished between "front" and "backstage" behaviors, the former being where "some aspects of the

FIGURE 1.7: Scarf vendor assisting a client.
CREDIT: Christopher Hutton

FIGURE 1.8: Silver Street vendor checking inventory.
CREDIT: Christopher Hutton

activity are expressly accentuated and others aspects, which might discredit
the fostered impression, are suppressed" (1959: 112). A greeting or the manner in which a vendor engages in negotiation over price could be considered

part of a vendor's "front," or "that part of the individual's performance which regularly functions in a general and fixed fashion to define the situation for those who observe the performance" (22). How audience members respond to the full spectrum of communicative aspects entailed by a social performance helps determine, in part, whether the performance is a success or failure. The expectation of consistency across interactions with shoppers and the importance of dramatic support in San Lorenzo are well illustrated in a remark made to me by one vendor concerning his spouse's talent for sales. "Look at how customers find my wife so likeable," he said, moving closer to where she was working to be sure she overheard him. "They ask for a discount, she gives them a smaller one, they don't argue, and then they embrace her. She draws them in with her clever ways." He added with a wink, "That's what she did to me, too!" In his example, customers request lower prices, and his wife responds with a figure higher than what was probably hoped for. Yet both parties are sufficiently satisfied with the negotiation process to carry the transaction to a successful conclusion. The request, the response, and even the hug are governed by a shared set of expectations about the experience of shopping in San Lorenzo.

Shared expectations about the appropriateness of certain behaviors as part of a marketplace performance also point to an embodied moral component: by claiming to be a particular kind of person, a vendor is exerting a moral demand that others "*ought* to see him as he 'is'" (Goffman 1959: 13; emphasis in original). Consider the case of another merchant, born in Florence, whose dignity was affronted by a shopper, also Florentine. The shopper pressed repeatedly for a "price for Florentines" less costly than the one written on the price tag. "*Signora*," the vendor bristled, "I charge the same prices to everyone. As a Florentine, no matter where someone comes from, I don't take anyone by the neck." This barbed retort evinced a desire to be seen as a straightforward businesswoman and, just as importantly, as a Florentine. It is striking that both the vendor and the customer pointed to their respective Florentine-ness during this interaction, even though it failed to meet the expectations of either one.

Knowing how to behave appropriately, like a "Florentine" in this particular case, is part of the body of skills and traditions that make up cultural knowledge. As Paul DiMaggio (1994: 27) has observed, "economic processes have an irreducible 'cultural' component." Pierre Bourdieu has argued that cultural knowledge is transmitted across generations as cultural capital (1977: 183–84) and that the possession of cultural capital bestows social advantages. These perspectives invite interesting comparison with more contemporary work by scholars in identity economics on the role of individual choice, conscious or unconscious, in selecting one's identity (Akerlof and Kranton 2010). Rodney Harrison (2010: 38) has noted that "if an individual can make a connection between their past and the heritage that is promoted as an aspect of their community's past, it gives them a connection they can use to 'purchase' privilege in social interactions." In the course of my own field experiences I have come to consider merchant comportment as an expression of embodied cultural capital that vendors can deploy and that carries value. Of course, as the example just cited demonstrates, sharing cultural identity, in that case as Florentines, does not always result in a positive interaction.

Richard Jenkins (2014: 27) has pointed out that "[w]e try to work out who strangers are even when we are merely observing them. We work at presenting ourselves, so that others will work out who we are along the lines that we wish them to." The importance of working at how we present ourselves may be why, in San Lorenzo today, the constituents of identities are under conscious scrutiny. The fact that *sanlorenzini* who face new competitors and customers refer so often to relative presence or absence of *fiorentinità* in San Lorenzo suggests that marketplace performances are useful points of entry both to some less-considered aspects of the impact of globalization on cultures as well as to how personal and collective identities reciprocally influence each other.

Some Dilemmas of *Fiorentinità*

The merchants whose stories I share describe their work identities in various ways. One is *bottegaio*. Traditionally, a *bottegaio* was the owner of an artisan workshop; now the term is often used vernacularly to refer to independent business owners. The ability to earn one's living as a *bottegaio* is highly esteemed in San Lorenzo. Signora Elena, for example, is the owner of Sabatone, a lively coffee bar. When I asked her to tell me about her work, she replied, "My establishment isn't a *bottega* [workshop], really, but to me it is like a *bottega*," she said. "I think of it as one. It is our place. So, even though we serve coffee and sandwiches, I see myself as a *bottegaia fiorentina*. I do business in a Florentine way *no matter what* [emphasis added]. I have been [doing things this way] for forty years." Signora Elena is among many *sanlorenzini* whose remarks point to intersections between her cultural and professional identities. She prefers to work, for example, in a "Florentine" way.

It is noteworthy that Signora Elena recognizes and emphasizes that there is a cultural component to the way that she comports herself at work. As a businesswoman in San Lorenzo, she is exposed to people from all over the world each day, tourists as well as foreign workers. One can encounter many tourists as well as *sanlorenzini* refreshing themselves at Sabatone Coffee Bar, for example. Living expenses around San Lorenzo are a bit lower than in some other parts of the city, a draw for tourists and immigrants alike.

Yet several issues associated with global flows of people, in particular recent immigration, rightly or wrongly have affected perceptions of this neighborhood in problematic ways. One is the fear of crime and the perceived growth of incivility generally. In mid-2007, for example, the neighborhood cinema just a few doors away from Signora Elena's coffee bar was slated for closure. Prior to going out of business, the manager called a press conference. He pointed out that enterprises up and down the street had been forced to shut their doors because fewer people now frequented neighborhood businesses and restaurants in the evening. He attributed patrons' absence to fear of encountering drunken vagrants, mostly undocumented immigrants, who may attempt to rob them. In making that statement, he was simply echoing a widely held sentiment. Warning his audience that a businessman had his eye on the spot for an adult cinema "in keeping with social conditions here," he suggested that even a few changes, such as more of a police presence and more public restrooms for clients of international telephone call centers, would improve livability: "Legal immigrants are far from home and have a right to be out in the evenings. For them, a call center is like a community center [*casa del popolo*] is to us. They deserve access to services just like we do."[12] The next morning, Lady Radio, a local station popularly known as "Violet Radio" among legions of fans of the Fiorentina soccer team, held a follow-up call-in show. A listener commented, "I am 40 years old. My father used to take me to San Lorenzo to shop for clothes and to buy boiled pork sandwiches at Da Nerbone." Da Nerbone, an eatery that specializes in traditional Florentine fare, has operated on the ground floor of the Central Market building since 1872. The moderator jumped in, noting that Da Nerbone still serves tasty sandwiches. "Yes, yes, it's still there," the caller opined, "but now San Lorenzo is the least Florentine part of the city. When I was a boy, it sounded Florentine. It felt Florentine. The *fiorentinità* is gone. What is it, now?"

The radio station caller's question, "What is [San Lorenzo], now?", was answered partly in the asking. San Lorenzo is different now. For the caller, the difference was a decline of *fiorentinità*. Remarks about *fiorentinità* on the radio, in letters to the editors of newspapers, in stump speeches by political candidates, on posters plastered on walls, and on placards carried at demonstrations reveal that many others, too, are concerned with its presence or absence.

Fiorentinità is a concept that clearly figures in the identity of many *sanlorenzini*. To understand its role, it is useful to consider it in terms of a

---

12 Call centers are small businesses that provide telephone and Internet services. Most call centers in San Lorenzo are managed by immigrant entrepreneurs and serve a largely immigrant and tourist clientele. *Casa del popolo* are community centers originally built by the Italian Communist Party (PCI) in the early twentieth century as an "alternative" to the Christian Democrats' use of the Catholic parishes and churches. One of their strategies was to construct centers offering various amenities at affordable prices and to provide a secular gathering place for non-elites (Kertzer 1980: 123–24).

process that has been called "identity amplification." Identity amplification refers to "the embellishment and strengthening of an existing identity" as part of identity work, in particular in aligning with social movements (Snow and McAdam 2000: 49). Snow and McAdam explain that "[i]n the language of role-identity theory, a change in the individual's identity salience hierarchy is affected.... The identity that has moved center stage was not foreign to the person's biography. Rather, it may have been a significant, moderately salient, or peripheral identity in one's past. Whatever the case, it has now been elevated to a position of salience...." (49). Thus an identity undergoing amplification is not new. Rather, for reasons specific to context, the amplified identity shifts to center stage.

Even while *fiorentinità* is important to identities, it resists being essentialized. Florentines themselves disagree about what it involves. In fact, it is much easier to start a conversation about *fiorentinità* by asking what it is not rather than what it is. For example, Florentines, like many Italians, posit distinctions between themselves and co-nationals that they often express in stereotypes. They jokingly point to their own *campanilismo*, a preference for habits and ways of being associated with one's place of origin, and are quick to note what they perceive as fundamental cultural differences between themselves and others.[13] Santo, a plumber who moved to Florence two decades ago and married into a Florentine family, explained to me,

> Italians all look the same outside. They have two eyes, a nose, a mouth. I do and so does he [he nodded at his brother-in-law, a Florentine standing nearby]. But inside [he tapped his head], the mentalities are different. Our identities are strong. I am Sicilian; we are cautious. Calabrians are hard [he pounded his fist in his hand for emphasis]. Closed. They don't talk. Ligurians don't spend money; they have short arms. Florentines are distant, aloof, probably even more closed than Calabrians. Hah! A little bit snobbish, and they curse the most!

After Santo finished speaking, his brother-in-law commented to me, "Come on! Look at how Sicilians wave their arms [when they talk]. Exaggerated!"

Michael Herzfeld has noted that stereotypes, when "embodied in increasingly stylized forms of self-presentation," can become self-confirming

---

13 Sociologist Lola Romanucci-Ross, whose family originated in the Le Marche region, notes that while growing up she was "provided with positive and negative role models from selected regions of Italy. I was told that it was good to emulate the Tuscans in the purity of their pronunciation of the language that Dante froze in print. They were hard-working and determined to succeed, though too materialistic and with more self-confidence than warranted. But the real negatives to be avoided included their acerbic tongues (too readily giving to blaspheming) and their emotions, pathologically cold. Also, in the most horrid ways, they know how to devastate others with cold contempt" (2006: 67).

(2004: 21). In that regard it is similarly important to contextualize how *fiorentinità* is differently conceptualized, portrayed, and deployed among Florentines. Not least among the reasons is that, as Sharon Macdonald (1993: 7) has emphasized, although identities are intangible social creations, "they are clearly not intangible in their effects and should not be regarded as epiphenomenal to more readily grasped economic and social phenomena." Macdonald is one of many researchers concerned with "the consequences of identity formation on the ground" (1993: 6) and who underscore that identities are flexible constructions with real-world consequences. *Fiorentinità* as a constituent of identities would be an example.

In that regard, it is intriguing that *fiorentinità* is a quality that is clearly becoming explicitly linked to some vendors' professional identity. George De Vos (2006: 13) has suggested that "[w]hen an individual acquires competence in a skill or profession, his or her primary commitment shifts to the mastery of a specific skill, or more generally to the social class of that profession.... This identity may be much stronger and more compelling than any national or ethnic allegiance." I do not suggest that objectification of *fiorentinità* as an element of work identity is an entirely new phenomenon; after all, Florentines are historically famous for their mercantile skill. Rather, I argue that *fiorentinità* as a constituent part of work identity has been elevated to greater salience in San Lorenzo in this time of rapid social transformation.

Herzfeld has pointed out, in writing about his experiences in the Roman district of Monti, that "[t]he fragility of social life evokes contrasts with a nostalgically reconstituted past.... The importance of such assertions is to decry the current situation ..." (2009: 21–22). Along those same lines, merchants and others in and about San Lorenzo refer to the presence or absence of *fiorentinità* through time. It is important to approach apparent nostalgia for an idealized Florentine past in San Lorenzo with a critical eye, because notions of the ideal are not uniform and the lens through which current transformations are viewed will influence how individuals feel about the neighborhood. For my sample, *fiorentinità* is associated with a time when local dialect was the rule and not the exception, when interactions among vendors and customers were more close-knit, familial, and predictable, when appropriate comportment among all parties was routine, and when the market served as much as a community center as it did as a place of commerce. Theirs is one view, but others exist that are addressed in this book as well. Interrogating the concept of *fiorentinità* helps us to understand better how identities are constructed and operationalized today, and the possible consequences.

Set in the heart of Florence, this book directs attention to the city's life blood: buying and selling. It explores what can be learned by observing how ordinary practices are changing and how people talk about change. It reveals some contradictions that characterize this neighborhood—magnificent and run down, bustling and empty, complex and simple, local and global—and uses them as springboards to questions about how identities and global forces interact. Chapter Two opens with a brief history of the neighborhood, including its engagement with globalizing processes. It also addresses the significance of *fiorentinità* to debates concerning the preservation of heritage. Chapter Three chronicles marketplace work life. It devotes particular attention to the dynamics of marketplace performances and how, according to some, they have been affected by immigration and tourism. Chapters Four and Five address contentious issues related to multicultural co-existence in this diverse neighborhood, and how they are related to efforts to reinvigorate *fiorentinità*. They also describe recent momentous changes in the marketplace's configuration and some reactions to it. The final chapter returns to *fiorentinità*, and identity in this marketplace specifically, suggesting that San Lorenzo remains, at least for now, a locale with both an identity and an identity crisis. The case of San Lorenzo helps us better to understand the evolution of personal and collective identities, the exercise of different forms of power, and how heritage may be created, maintained, and transformed. For all of these reasons, and others besides, what is happening in San Lorenzo will continue to be of interest in this city, throughout Italy, and beyond.

CHAPTER TWO

A MERCANTILE NEIGHBORHOOD ACROSS TIME

One afternoon a customer I was serving at the market, surprised by my American accent, volunteered that she grew up in San Lorenzo and married an American. She had moved to the United States in the 1970s and was back to visit her mother. I asked how she thought San Lorenzo today compared with her marketplace memories. She sighed and commented:

> This market has changed. The merchants have changed, too. To be honest, I resent it. The flavor has changed. Well, there *used* to be flavor [her emphasis]! I used to shop for school clothes here. I haven't looked closely at all of these products yet. I don't know if they are artisanal or imported, but it certainly isn't as personally involved as it used to be. I feel like I hardly belong here. We have outdoor markets in Columbus, Ohio, too, you know. They feel like San Lorenzo does now. I don't know why I am surprised and resentful to see this market change. I don't even live here; maybe that makes me a tourist and not a San Lorenzo person. But I am sure that Italians resent the change.

As in many instances when *sanlorenzini* comment on San Lorenzo, this woman's remarks focused on change rather than continuity. Jacopo, the fruit and vegetable vendor introduced in Chapter One, is another case in point. I met Jacopo in 2005, drawn to his stand by cheeky posters about not selling to anyone who was not a Fiorentina soccer fan. As he transferred wild strawberries into paper sacks for me, I mentioned that I hoped someday to write a book about the market. Jacopo began pointing out changes:

> I've been working here full-time since 1986, but even while I was in school I used to come and help my grandfather, especially in the summers. It was like a big family at the market then. Boys played soccer in the piazza out back, where lots of fruit vendors used to be located. Ladies would pull up

chairs and watch. Everyone talked and talked and talked. Everyone was calling out to everyone else. No one had very much; we eat better now. But *sanlorenzini* were always bringing each other something or giving one another a taste of something. San Lorenzo *com'era* (as it was).

He turned his attention to an elderly customer who was eyeing some peaches. "Isn't it true, Ma'am?" She nodded in agreement.

In fact, almost every Florentine with whom I have spoken about San Lorenzo reports that it used to feel different, specifically more congenial. At the extreme, some *sanlorenzini* claim the marketplace has become nearly unrecognizable. One *sanlorenzino* scoffed when asked if he would attend the neighborhood's annual watermelon feast on August 10, the patron saint's feast day. "I went to the watermelon feast when it had *fiorentinità* and I felt like I belonged," he replied. "Who are these people? Now it is no place for me."

The conflicted feelings that some *sanlorenzini* clearly espouse about this place originate in the lack of fit between their past and current experiences, nostalgic ideals, and present-day realities in this setting. While San Lorenzo is a neighborhood identified with mercantile pursuits, the tone of life and trade is shaped and reshaped by those who work, live, and shop there. Those populations are changing. This chapter sets the stage for a deeper understanding of change with a short introduction to the neighborhood's remarkable history and some of its residents.

FIGURE 2.1: San Lorenzo Night celebration, 1961.
CREDIT: Torrini Fotogiornalismo

A City of Merchants

Florence is often described as a city of art. But it can be characterized just as well as a city of merchants. Florentines today have inherited and maintained their ancestors' reputation as skilled businessmen and businesswomen. The city was already a center of international commerce in medieval times, and the merchants of Florence were powerful forces in the larger European economy throughout the Renaissance. Concerning the legacy of these "merchant princes," a nineteenth-century writer commented, "In Florence the root of roots was trade. [The city's] real builders were not its great architects, artists and Barons, but its traders. Its *Libro d'oro* [sic] is literally a record of successful merchants, whose highest maxim was to buy where they could buy the cheapest and sell where they could sell dearest" (Jarves 1881).[1] Fifteenth-century scholar Gregorio Dati suggested that Florentines developed this acumen in response to the limitations of the city's geographic setting:

> [A reason why Florentines are more prosperous than their neighbors] is this: because the city of Florence is located in a naturally wild and sterile place.... no matter how hard it is worked it cannot give enough for its inhabitants to live from.... So, it is necessary for some time now that Florentines ... have gone ... to other lands and provinces, and countries to make their fortune before returning to Florence ... and travelling through all the kingdoms of the world and [of] Christians and infidels ... an even greater desire to see and to acquire has come to them; and the one has increased the desire for the other, so that whoever is not a merchant and hasn't searched the world and seen people of foreign nations and returned with goods to his homeland is considered nothing. And this love has so inflamed their souls that, for some time, it has seemed that this is what they are naturally born for ... behaving as they do, they are capable of increasing their riches indefinitely and their happiness (Dati 1902 [orig. 1405?]: 59–60).

Among the best known of Florence's Renaissance merchants was Giovanni di Paolo Rucellai (1403–81). A textile manufacturer, he belonged to the most powerful of the guilds that controlled trade and otherwise wielded influence in the thriving city-state. Rucellai perhaps spoke for merchants in Florence across the centuries when he opined, "It's generally said, and I agree with it, that earning and spending are among the greatest pleasures that men enjoy in this life. I myself ... have had the greatest pleasure and satisfaction from both" (Hunt 1999: 14). Even in Rucellai's time, the area in which San Lorenzo is located had already achieved a reputation as a place for commerce.

---

1 The *Libro d'Oro Della Nobiltà Italiana* is a catalog of members of the Italian nobility. See: http://www.collegio-araldico.it/english/librodoroeng.htm.

San Lorenzo in Medieval and Medicean Times

The subject of this book is San Lorenzo as it is experienced by some people who work or live there now. To understand their experience, however, it is important to keep in mind that this part of the city has a history that spans nearly a thousand years. This particular neighborhood has, in fact, maintained its standing as a lively site for buying and selling for about 800 years. History continues to shape the expectations of many *sanlorenzini* and figures in their responses to the impacts of globalization.

The story of San Lorenzo literally begins at the steps of the church from which the neighborhood takes its name. Consecrated in 393, San Lorenzo was Florence's first recorded church. At the time of its founding, the church was located outside the city's original Roman wall. It served as the Bishop of Florence's seat until the early eleventh century. Although the San Lorenzo Church deteriorated physically over time, it was renovated and re-consecrated in the twelfth century and became the favorite of the general Florentine public. In recognition of the special place it occupied in the heart and history of the city's faithful, a papal bull issued in 1197 declared San Lorenzo to be "Mother and Head of the Florentine Ecclesia." A second city wall completed soon thereafter extended beyond the original one and contained the Basilica of San Lorenzo within it. It became known as Florence's "Medieval Wall."

Its popularity notwithstanding, the church was eventually eclipsed by Florence's grand cathedral Santa Maria del Fiore, begun in 1296 and completed in 1436. By the start of the fifteenth century, San Lorenzo Church had again fallen into ruin. Wealthy merchant Giovanni di Bicci de' Medici (1360–1429), whose descendants later ruled the city, provided funds for the church's second renovation. Filippo Brunelleschi (1377–1446), whose other commissions included creating the cathedral's remarkable dome, was the architect in charge. He executed the renovation in what was then the new "Renaissance" style. Giovanni di Bicci's son, Cosimo (1389–1464), continued family sponsorship of San Lorenzo and chose to build his home near the church. That edifice, known today as the Medici Riccardi Palace, was completed in the 1440s.

Over time, the San Lorenzo Church became ever more associated with the de' Medici family. In 1518 Michelangelo Buonarotti (1475–1564), whose masterworks already included his iconic statue of David and Rome's Sistine Chapel frescos, was commissioned to design the new sacristy, an adjacent library, and a cloister. A century after Michelangelo's death, a "Chapel of Princes" was added to the rear of the church complex. A bell tower was erected in the eighteenth century. Today lines of schoolchildren and tourists can often be found waiting their turn to explore the complex or gazing at a statue of Anna Maria Luisa de' Medici (1667–1743), daughter of Cosimo III (1642–1726) and last direct descendant of Giovanni di Bicci de' Medici, which is located in the tiny garden directly behind the Chapel of Princes.

Countless scholarly works are devoted to the architecture of the San Lorenzo Church, artistic treasures within it, and activities and genealogies of notable parish families. Far fewer address ordinary life in this neighborhood across the centuries. Nicolas Eckstein, writing about neighborhoods in Renaissance Florence generally, offered a suggestion that could aptly be extended to their study today as well: "It is in trying to trace and understand the origin of ... overlapping 'microcommunities,' that one can best hope to understand the culture of the [Florentine] neighborhood" (2006: 221). Eckstein continued, "Florentine neighborhood culture was inseparable from urban space, but geography is not the sole creator of relationships, and it should be treated as a necessary constituent and not a sufficient cause of sociability.... Extended family relationships that were based in neighborhoods could overlap with the social contract between neighbors more generally; such bonds could in turn intersect and fuse with the many commercial and professional relationships that proliferated at the local level" (221).

To understand neighborhood culture and the relationships among San Lorenzo's microcommunities, it is therefore necessary to know something about the formal and informal organization of urban space over time. Renaissance Florentines across social ranks were influenced by, and in turn exerted influence over, specific urban zones. These zones were divided and subdivided to accommodate administrative, religious, and other needs. During the Renaissance, Florence was divided into six administrative sections. Administrative sixths were subdivided into administrative wards, or sub-districts. San Lorenzo parish formed part of the city's administrative sixth known as "Cathedral's Gate" for its proximity to Santa Maria del Fiore. San Lorenzo Church and its immediate environs were located in the local ward of the "Gold Lion." Eckstein explains, "For citizens either wealthy or well-connected enough to have a stake in the political life of the city, the local ward, the *gonfalone*, was perhaps the most important neighborhood institution.... It is thus no accident that unofficial discussion about the *gonfaloni* ... was usually cast in terms of the powerful families who sought to control the political life of their immediate neighborhood" (2006: 221–22).[2]

Not all city residents were affiliated with powerful families, of course, and therefore those who were not were unlikely to play a role in administrative ward politics proper. Instead, they channeled their civic activities into voluntary festive brigades or plebian kingdoms referred to as "powers." These so-called powers usually comprised territories smaller than administrative wards. David Rosenthal suggests that by the late Renaissance these jurisdictions, too, were "fixtures in the Florentines' mental map of their polis" (Rosenthal 2006: 162).

---

2 For more on the *gonfalone* system, see Kent and Kent (1982).

The Gold Lion ward where San Lorenzo Church is located contained several different festive kingdoms. Among them were the "Kingdom of Gold," "Song and Dance," and "The Gridiron." The Kingdom of Gold was located near what is now the Central Market piazza. The self-designated "vassals" of that kingdom were employed mostly in the production of gold lace for the caps of Florentine noblewomen. The officials of these plebian kingdoms were not craftsmen themselves; they were porters, sweepers, oven-stokers, and other unskilled laborers associated with workshops (Ciabani 1998: 21–22).

The Song and Dance plebian kingdom was composed of textile laborers. Roberto Ciabani surmises that the kingdom took its name from a Turkish word for noise, celebration, and confusion (1998: 22). Renaissance Florentine poet Lapo Minucci described the subjects of Song and Dance in disparaging terms, alleging that "although born and raised in Florence [they] are different from other Florentines in their customs and in their speech … they eat every kind of filth like cats, dogs, and spoiled fish and meat: they drink every sort of unregulated wine … in short they are a people to themselves" (Ciabani 1994: 62). Song and Dance's legacy in San Lorenzo is visible even today in art commissioned under its sponsorship. The "Tabernacle of the Madonna," a decorated wall niche on what is known today as National Street, houses a painting of the Virgin Mary commissioned by members. The tabernacle is visible from many market stands on Silver Street. Tourists and some residents can be seen refilling water bottles at the public fountain added beneath the painting in 1522.

A third plebian kingdom in San Lorenzo used the church itself as its convocation point. The Gridiron kingdom took its name from the method by which Saint Lawrence was popularly believed to have met his martyrdom in 258—being roasted alive.[3] According to a late-sixteenth-century account, the Gridiron actually crowned its potentate inside the San Lorenzo Church and then carried him outdoors into the church piazza "with great noise and joy, with drums, trumpets and bells …" (Rosenthal 2006: 164).

In time, the *gonfalone* system was abandoned and the plebian kingdoms vanished. In the seventeenth century, Florence was re-subdivided into administrative fourths or *quartieri*. San Lorenzo was apportioned to the *quartiere* of Santa Maria Novella. Today there are officially five *quartieri*; San Lorenzo is considered part of Quartiere I, Historic Center. That there were formerly four quarters of this city is remembered with the annual Calcio Fiorentino match, where residents or representatives of the original *quartiere*, dressed in sixteenth-century garb in their quarter's colors, compete in an early and

---

3 While some believe that Saint Lawrence was burned alive by the Prefect of Rome, Valerian, most historians and other scholars claim he was beheaded. The annual Perseid meteor shower is called the "Tears of Saint Lawrence" because its peak activity coincides with the Feast of Saint Lawrence on August 10.

very aggressive version of soccer. There are now 16 jurisdictionally distinct administrative districts in Florence; a *quartiere* today is more of a notional community or "neighborhood." Early twentieth-century Florentine novelist Vasco Pratolini, for example, begins *Il Quartiere*, his tale of hardscrabble life in and around Florence's Santa Croce Church, with the proprietary remark "We liked our Quarter" (1960: 5).

As in Pratolini's day, Florentines continue to profess strong partiality toward their own *quartiere*. In light of their sentimental attachments, it is all the more striking that people elsewhere in this city sometimes refer to San Lorenzo as the "heart" of Florence and to the vendors of a half-century ago as "real Florentines." Such statements are often followed, predictably, by remarks about the marketplace's transformation, rarely for the better. But even if some react unfavorably to what they consider significant changes in this environment, the San Lorenzo Market itself is the product of change, as the next section details.

Old, New, and Newer Markets

Like Poldo, Mister Violet, and the Florentine Elvis (among the local notables first mentioned in Chapter One), the San Lorenzo Market is easily recognizable. Where the San Lorenzo neighborhood ends and the next neighborhood begins is less obvious. San Lorenzo extends like an open palm across a roughly two-square-mile northern area near the main train station, Santa Maria Novella. It forms part of Florence's historic center and edges the piazza where the city's cathedral is located. The summit of the cathedral's fourteenth-century bell tower is clearly visible above the canvas awnings of many outdoor carts.

San Lorenzo Market has played a fundamental role in life in this city for more than a hundred years, yet it is a relative newcomer to the historic center. From Roman times through most of the nineteenth century, the city's main marketplace was situated a short distance away, where an ancient Roman forum was once located. Staley writes that "the earliest historical record gives the year 1079 as the date when the *Mercato Vecchio* [Old Market] received its name," although it appears that the market was in existence 40 years earlier, and possibly longer (1906: 445). In the early fifteenth century, a column topped with a female figure personifying "Abundance" was erected to mark the Roman city center.[4] A different sculpture, also of "Abundance," is found in nearly the same spot today. Now, rather than butchers and farmers

---

4 For more on the history of the statue and an interpretation of what it may have represented to Renaissance Florentines, see Wilk (1986).

hawking vegetables, she is surrounded by upscale cafés, street performers including opera singers, nose flute players, and men and women covered with white body paint who pose like statues, as well as a Hard Rock Cafe.

Throughout the Middle Ages and the Renaissance, that marketplace, which has been called "the most venerable site in Florence" (Staley 1906: 445), was loud, lively, and lewd. The wares offered for sale and the habits of those who bought and sold them were fondly and colorfully described in a fourteenth-century poem by Antonio Pucci (1310–88). In Pucci's estimation, Florence's ancient marketplace was the "Fairest in the World" and "[carried] off the prize from every other *piazza*" (Horner and Horner 1877: 161). According to Pucci,

> There never was so noble a garden
> As that presented by the old market
> Which feasts the eyes and taste of the Florentines …
> Such is the grandeur of this market
> That it has four churches at the four corners,
> And at every corner are two streets.[5]

As Florence's population expanded, so did its capacity for trade. As a result, a new marketplace, used primarily by textile merchants and money-changers, grew up nearby. Afterward, Florence's ancient commercial area came to be known as the "Old Market" to distinguish it from this "New Market" (Staley 1906: 462). A free-standing roofed stone portico was added in the 1500s to protect merchants and their wares. On occasion, the battle chariot of the Florentines was displayed there. Later, the New Market was embellished with a so-called Scandal Stone, actually a marble inset in the form of a chariot wheel in the center of the floor. Those who could not pay their debts faced public humiliation there.[6] Over time, the New Market received even more flourishes. One favorite was a public fountain adorned with a copy of Pietro Tacca's (1577–1640) bronze statue of a boar, completed in 1612. The New Market, also occasionally called the "Straw Market," derives its present-day nickname, "the Piglet," or Porcellino, from that statue. Crowds of tourists can nearly always be found jostling for turns to rub the piglet's snout and slip a coin between its parted lips, a popular superstition that purportedly results in a return to Florence.

---

5 Antonio Pucci, "Le proprietà di Mercato Vecchio," included in Horner and Horner (1877) and Brucker (1983).

6 Staley (1906: 464) reports that "bankrupts" were tied to a post erected on that spot and beaten publicly. Local anecdote today suggests that debtors' britches were lowered to below their buttocks and they were compelled to sit on the stone before a jeering crowd of onlookers. The "scandal stone" is still visible today.

As is the case in San Lorenzo today, a cross-section of society would certainly have congregated in the Old and New Markets during the Renaissance. Gene Brucker notes that "[b]y their speech and dress, the individuals in this crowd revealed their provenance, social rank, and occupation" (1983: 41). Peasants offered wares to the serving-women of Florentine families while "respectable men and their wives arrived to watch the scene, dazzled" (Welch 2005: 33).[7] Yet even the poet Pucci, who described its charms in verse, tempered his panegyric to the Old Market with warnings, because pleasure and danger were available in equal measure (Welch 2005: 33). In this crowded venue, order could shift quickly to disorder, and "petty quarrels could quickly disintegrate into warring factions" (33).

The Old and New Markets have been described as the "lungs" of "the Commerce of Florence" (Staley 1906: 444). Of the two, only the New Market survives. The Old Market was demolished near the end of the nineteenth century as part of the massive urban renovation program launched when Florence was designated to serve as temporary capital of the Kingdom of Italy beginning in 1865. Florence's largest public square, the Piazza Repubblica, is now located in the space once occupied by the Old Market. The New Market was insufficiently large for Florence's needs, however, so three additional marketplaces were proposed: one was to be built in the Sant'Ambrogio neighborhood near Santa Croce Church, another in the San Frediano neighborhood across the Arno River, and the third and largest would be erected in San Lorenzo.

When those three markets were envisioned, San Lorenzo was a neighborhood of less than stellar repute. Residents mostly inhabited low-ceilinged apartments in attached buildings that flanked narrow, crowded lanes and alleyways. Then, as now, ground floors usually functioned as shops. Sources have described San Lorenzo's old streets as *camaldoli* (Bianca 1995: 81). A descriptor that does not translate easily, the term *camaldoli* may derive from the name of a religious order that operated a monastery in a squalid part of what is now the neighborhood of San Frediano (Bencistà 2001: 95; Brucker 1967: 123). Eckstein notes, "Camaldoli was known in early times as a dumping ground for refuse," later on as a place where "paupers were buried 'like beasts,' and its status [was that of] a working class neighborhood on the fringes of civilized development ..." (2006: 227). The phrase *"camaldoli* of San Lorenzo" suggests that these two marginal areas of the city, one "at the fringes of civilized development" and the other being San Lorenzo, were

---

7 Staley describes the Old Market as "the well" of every Florentine's life, "the fulcrum of his fortune, and the show-ground of his pride" (1906: 451). As for the scene in the market, Staley claims that conflict often broke out "between class and class and trade and trade." Furthermore, "riots in the Market were normal events" and "prominent families and their adherents were involved in a grim death struggle" as rival trades fought "in battle-royal over the merest incident" (453–54).

somewhat equivalent in the sense that their inhabitants were characterized as people who engaged in behaviors considered outside the norms of the local elite.

To make room for San Lorenzo's new market building and piazza, four San Lorenzo housing blocks were demolished and their inhabitants resettled, mostly across the Arno River. A commission to design the Central Market building was awarded to the noted architect Giuseppe Mengoni (1829–77), who had just completed Milan's award-winning complex Galleria Vittorio Emanuele II. Mengoni's plans for Florence's Central Market were similarly ambitious, leading to its eventual acclaim as the city's most prestigious nine-teenth-century building; it would have appeared very grand indeed at its inauguration. The architecture that surrounds the Central Market is mostly fifteenth- and sixteenth-century four- and five-story gray, ocher, or honey-colored attached stucco buildings with tiny windows. Mengoni set his market building visually apart by renovating the buildings to the left and right including adding porticos. The Central Market building stands in the center like a palace. Its imposing stone walls were, in fact, intended to evoke the grandeur of the nearby Medici Family Palace. The market's roof is another style entirely. It is a gleaming latticework of metal and glass that illuminates the interior space and engenders a feeling of strolling outdoors even though one is inside. The ironwork includes softening floral flourishes that draw the eye upward. To shoppers who patronized its merchants a dozen decades ago, Mengoni's building may have called to mind Paris's Eiffel Tower, another urban marvel under construction at roughly the same time.

The Central Market was intended for the sale of meat and fish, and its merchants primarily offered cheap cuts that were within the means of the working class. Those selections included the staples of what is now called Florentine "poor kitchen" (or peasant) cuisine, such as tripe and abomasum, the cow's fourth stomach. Some butchers and fishmongers today continue to work upon marble countertops installed in 1892 when the market became operational.

The original building did not include space for greengrocers. They labored year-round outside beneath a free-standing iron portico in the adjoining Market Piazza. That iconic iron serpentine portico no longer exists; it was dismantled after the city approved construction of an upper story for the market in 1976. Fruit and vegetable vendors were relocated to that new space in the early 1980s. In keeping with local usage, this volume refers to the entrance floor as the market's "ground floor" and the upper story as the "first floor." A few years ago, the first floor was again closed for renovation. Some greengrocers, including Jacopo, rented small niches on the ground floor. Others were relocated behind the building, to the piazza where their nineteenth-century predecessors had worked. Rather than being somewhat protected from the outside elements by an iron portico, however, they had to be satisfied with space inside an enormous canvas tent close to an assemblage of industrial-size dumpsters.

From Traveling to Stationary Peddlers

This relocation of fruit and vegetable vendors from indoors to the piazza could be viewed as in keeping with a Florentine tradition: city residents have long frequented peddlers who conducted trade outdoors. Throughout this city's history, however, local authorities have generally taken a dim view of outdoor vendors. In the Renaissance, for example, they were considered a threat to social and moral order. Pucci's poem further described roving female traders who "might give some fright" (Hibbert 2004: 58) and who "fight throughout the day over two dried chestnuts calling each other whores.... And they are always filling their baskets with fruit to their advantage" (Welch 2005: 34). Traveling or "ambulant vendors" were historically treated by authorities as "exterior rather than as intrinsic to the social body of the city state" (Brucker 1983: 40). Legislation was created to curb their business and the sounds of their salesmanship. A statute of 1325 directed at Jewish vendors stipulated, "None are to go about the city crying 'Gold and Silver': As infidel youths wander selling … they commit many, many thefts in buying and selling … therefore we order that no person should dare or presume to go about the city … shouting … out such venal things" (Brucker 1983: 42). One argument in favor of the construction of a large Central Market building in San Lorenzo, in fact, was that it would allow for large numbers of peddlers to be collocated. Civic officials considered it advantageous because centralization would reduce cart traffic, improve public hygiene, and make it easier to oversee this particular commercial activity. The apprehension that ambulant vending provoked among civic officials in Florence in the past can be compared in some ways to the anxiety it induces among them today, as subsequent chapters reveal.

The Central Market building has now been operational for 125 years. It did not take construction of this impressive building to persuade enterprising vendors that San Lorenzo was an excellent base of operations, however. At least by the Renaissance, peddlers were already conducting business in the church's vicinity; the church grounds have doubled as spaces for an open-air market for 500 years. Bygone clergy members' reputed willingness to grant indulgences—special pardons—to parishioners who came to church on market days may have been among conditions that Renaissance peddlers found particularly appealing (Sieni 1995: 50).

Photographs of nineteenth-century Florence provide images of San Lorenzo vendors offering clothes, housewares, and other items outside the church. Some show merchandise hung directly upon the church's exterior

FIGURE 2.2: San Lorenzo church and vendors, 1915.
CREDIT: Alinari/ArtResource NY

walls and it is said that, at that time, customers pitched stones to indicate items that interested them. One epochal photograph depicts a peddler posed with a display of sparrows secured by threads to a perch. For a coin, he would signal one of them to dive into a box and procure a slip of paper with a fortune written upon it. Others show wagons laden with merchandise rolling past the entrance of the then newly completed Central Market building.

With the opening of the Central Market, the city began requiring San Lorenzo vendors to be licensed. While stories abound concerning who was given licenses and why, there are two dominant narratives. One is that early licenses were given to former convicts at no cost. The reason was that potential recidivists, when conveniently collocated, were simpler to keep an eye on. The second narrative is that early licensees were mostly unemployed Florentine military veterans who received permits at a reduced cost. The difference between the versions is significant: the first suggests that San Lorenzo vendors have always been marginal to Florentine society, while the second dignifies former military men who chose to pursue livelihoods there. In version one, vendors are potentially dangerous persons; in version two, they are patriotic fellow citizens. Which version prevails depends on who is telling the story.

Regardless of who originally was there, and why, the Central Market has been fundamental to the lives of *sanlorenzini* for over a hundred years.

FIGURE 2.3: Rear view of the Central Market and market piazza, 1958.
CREDIT: Torrini Fotogiornalismo

It eventually came to be considered the "Pulse Point of Florentine Life" (Giannelli 2007: 38). The realms of the sacred and the profane have traditionally cohabited comfortably there. For example, some enterprising Florentines eventually built shops that were attached directly to the exterior walls of San Lorenzo Church. These structures were not removed until well into the twentieth century. A 2004 visitors' guide even describes the church

FIGURE 2.4: Shopping in San Lorenzo, 1958.
CREDIT: Torrini Fotogiornalismo

piazza as this neighborhood's "commercial entrance" (Chiarini 2004: 65). The economic centerpiece, of course, is the Central Market building. When I began this project in 2005, space was apportioned inside the building for 200 enterprises over two floors (although not all spaces were occupied). The vendors sold meat, fish, wine, condiments, and produce. There were coffee bars, casual restaurants, bread shops, and a fresh pasta stand. Increasing numbers of vendors also offered *turistica*, at least as a sideline. *Turistica* are items primarily selected to appeal to the hundreds of thousands of domestic and international visitors who enter this building each year. Examples include "travel-sized" beribboned packets containing dried porcini mushrooms, soup or pesto mixes, and toppings for toasted bread. Miniature bottles of wine or liquor, flamboyantly colored pasta, small jars of local honey, and some vacuum-packed foods are also considered *turistica*. One Central Market business proudly displayed the story that appeared a few years ago in an English-language gourmet magazine with an accompanying sign in English noting that theirs is a "Celebrity Store" with its own brand of herb and spice packets-to-go.

Surveys conducted in 2007 and 2008 by four of my undergraduate research assistants determined that about 20 per cent of Central Market businesses stocked at least some *turistica*. Furthermore, 30 per cent of indoor vendors advertised or provided price lists in English, and another 10 per cent advertised in Japanese. These percentages increased slightly over the two-year period and have continued gradually to rise. The ground floor today still looks much as it did in 2005, with the exception of a handful of greengrocers who have relocated there. The first floor has been completely transformed, however. In the space formerly occupied by greengrocers and flower vendors there are now wine bars and pubs, big-screen televisions, upscale restaurants, a cooking school, and an entire shop devoted mostly to the sale of made-in-Italy packaged food items that could be considered *turistica*. The first floor is advertised to the English-speaking public as a place for "Street Food with Comfort"; many visitors characterize it as a "food court."

Promotional materials have referred to the Central Market as "a small town made of shops." In fact it is one small town of shops nestled within another, like a pair of Russian dolls. Just outside the doors of the Central Market's interior are dozens more small shops, eateries including ethnic take-aways, fast-food chain outlets, pubs, supermarkets, and at least half a dozen Internet cafés and international call centers. In addition, there are hundreds of individual ambulant vendors working from licensed stands directly on the streets.

These independent market stands of San Lorenzo line a half dozen neighborhood streets like domino tiles. The outdoor market footprint has grown gradually, eventually amalgamating with the open-air market that surrounded the church until 2014. Growth in the number of stands over the past 30 years in particular has been dramatic. One Florentine in his early fifties commented about the market's growth, "Today I see almost nothing but carts bursting with leather coats along the porticos on either side of the Central Market. When I was a boy coming here with my parents there weren't any at all. There, under that portico, I remember a button seller, somebody selling socks, somebody else was selling dried salted cod—cheap food for people who worked hard. There was space to move around and there was also variety here. It wasn't crowded with *banchi*[8] all selling the same things like it is now."

Overcrowding and product redundancy are issues that affect more than simply the tone of the market to which the interviewee referred. They are significant obstacles for many vendors who must try to outcompete a merchant selling the very same product, sometimes only one meter away. How vendors interact with customers and other vendors has been affected as a result. How they have been affected, and the implications, are addressed in Chapter Four.

Over time, outdoor vendors replaced their horse-drawn wagons with wheeled carts, called *barroccio* in Florentine dialect, or, in Italian, *bancarella* or *banco* for short. The plural of *banco* is *banchi*. Vendors' *banchi* today do not resemble the wagons or the early pushcarts of the past. Instead, *banchi* are rolling crates that open to reveal display cases outfitted with drawers and shelves. Luxury models are motorized and have rubber tires. Inventory ranges

---

8 For a definition of *banco/banchi*, see below.

FIGURE 2.5: Purse vendor near the San Lorenzo church, 1959.
CREDIT: Torrini Fotogiornalismo

from ceramics to tapestry, writing paper, gloves, chess sets, knickknacks, and more. Many items on sale in the San Lorenzo market are identical to those that can be purchased across town at the New Market, although San Lorenzo offers greater selection. Still, vending in San Lorenzo's lacks the cachet of working in the New Market. One vendor explained:

> People make a judgment about you as soon as you say that you have a *banco* in San Lorenzo. Once, I was walking around the stands at the *Festa dell' Unità* in the Fortress.[9] I complimented a guy on his *banco* and he replied, "This isn't a *banco*; these are artisanal goods." He told me he

---

9 The Fortress to which the speaker refers is the Fortezza da Basso, originally Fortezza di San Giovanni Battista, erected in the early sixteenth century. Part of the fortress is built directly into Florence's thirteenth-century city wall. Today the edifice is used as a convention and fair space.

usually worked in the Piglet. I said that I sold artisanal goods, too, but in San Lorenzo. "That isn't a market," he said. "That's nothing." I asked him if he had ever been there and he said no. I was so angry! So I asked, "What do you know about it, if you haven't been there?" He apologized, and I said, "Listen, the New Market isn't the only historic market. San Lorenzo has a history." Thirty years ago this ugly thing would not have been said to me. Sure, I am a San Lorenzo vendor, but 30 years ago San Lorenzo was the market of the Florentines!

Diversity in the Most Cosmopolitan Part of the City

I made reference earlier to Gregorio Dati, who wrote about the appetite for trade of Florentines 500 years ago. Dati suggested that travel was critical to sharpening the skills of Florentine merchants; some spent nearly their entire lives in other cities in Italy or abroad. Their experiences were not always pleasant. As the Florentine merchant Bernardo Davanzati wrote about his work life in Venice, "There is always someone ready to make trouble for us poor foreigners" (Hibbert 2004: 25). Dati might not have been surprised to learn that large numbers of non-Florentines now come to this city to advance their own abilities at trade. Commerce in Florence is constant, but it is not the provenance of Florentines only. Work in the commercial sector is among the factors that have led this city to become a destination of choice for large numbers of immigrants.

Immigrants at work in San Lorenzo are not a new phenomenon. Signora Sabrina, owner of a fashionable hair salon patronized by *sanlorenzini*, commented, "Immigrants have always come here because of the market; some come from down there [Southern Italy], and some are foreigners. There were already foreigners working here when I was growing up. Not this many, but some. Being near the train station is the reason why ours is the most cosmopolitan part of the city." Among Southern Italians who migrated north and found success in San Lorenzo is Niccolò, who arrived from the southern region of Basilicata more than 20 years ago. Asked why he came to Florence, Niccolò, a purveyor of quality leather purses and briefcases at a Silver Street *banco*, replied, "There wasn't work in my town, but I could have gone someplace else. I came to Florence because I had a teacher who was Florentine. He talked about the city, showed us pictures. I wanted to live in that beautiful place. Working at San Lorenzo is hard, but sometimes, when I walk along the [Arno] river and look around, I feel inspired. This is a remarkable city! Or, anyway, it was and could be again."

Sabrina, born in the 1960s, pointed out that non-Italians have also worked in San Lorenzo since she was a girl. She referred mostly to men who formed part of two earlier influxes. It is said that many Greek immigrants opened *banchi* there soon after World War II. Even larger numbers of Persians arrived in the late 1970s and early 1980s, around the time of the Iranian revolution. Many of those Greeks and Persians eventually became naturalized Italian citizens. Yet, as Sabrina pointed out, the number of foreigners in San Lorenzo has lately undergone more conspicuous growth. That increase is part of a much larger national trend that began in the 1970s and accelerated thereafter (King 1993; King and Andall 1999). Between 1989 and 1999, the number of resident foreigners in Italy doubled (Grillo and Pratt 2002: 5). By the early 1990s, Tuscany was already among the five Italian regions with the highest concentrations of foreigners (Cole 1997: 4). Immigrants come to Italy from myriad countries, including some in North Africa and Eastern Europe. Significant numbers have also journeyed there from Southeast Asia, Latin America, and South Asia (Cole 1997: 5). The regional population of Tuscany now also includes large numbers of Chinese (Krause 2005: 17) and West Africans, in particular Senegalese.

Not all foreigners come to Florence seeking work, obviously. Many come for pleasure, including the pleasure of learning, as I did. For many centuries the city was an important stop on the "grand tour" that capped the education of European elites. Today it is the world's most popular non-anglophone destination for North American students on study-abroad programs, and highly sought out as a destination for many types of study tours (Di Giovine 2009: 152). Throughout the 10 years that I co-directed a summer program in Florence, nearly every student wrote on their evaluation that four weeks was not long enough to experience a city that was, for so many, life-changing. Three returned immediately for a semester or year of study, and another is now conducting his doctoral dissertation research in San Lorenzo on Latin American immigrant mutual-aid networks.

Florence is also usually found at or near the top of travelers' surveys of the most desirable places in the world to vacation, partly the result of the far-reaching efforts to "re-launch" tourism that began in the 1950s. Strategies for promoting the city included its leaders "assiduously" courting representatives of the United States (Miller 2002: 61). By the 1960s, tourism had become "the industry that carried all others" (150), and it remains so today. Dozens of travel guides and Internet sites now list the open-air market and Central Market building among the city's touristic highlights. Selling to tourists is an activity upon which most outdoor merchants and many of their indoor counterparts depend. What is perhaps unexpected is the personal satisfaction that many derive from encounters with foreigners. Cristoforo, a leather merchant originally from Iran, describes interactions with foreign visitors as among the most pleasurable aspects of his profession. He explains, "Here, from my business, I can only see San Lorenzo. Here, from San Lorenzo, I can't see mountains, oceans, or other countries. But in San Lorenzo the world comes to me. It is traveling without buying a plane ticket. I don't see countries, but I see cultures. Cultures come here, and this is how I increase my knowledge. Meeting people from all over the world is what makes working here an education." Niccolò, the purse vendor, has a similar view: "There might be someplace in the world yet to send a tourist to San Lorenzo, but I can't imagine where. There was even a tour group from the South Pacific walking around here last month. I like my work because it is not just about the sale. Sure I want to sell things, certainly, but I learn about the world by talking with visitors. I am proud that someone from the South Pacific came to my business and took one of my purses home. I selected it, I offered it, and she chose to buy it from me." Niccolò's comment about this tourist's purchase from him is, in fact, very astute. Customers' preferences for particular types of shopping experiences constitute a variable that propels some vendors to adjust their marketplace performances in ways that underscore the social and cultural complexities of operating a business in the market.

Choosing the Right Vendor

A benefit of working as a sales assistant as part of my participant-observation methodology was having opportunities to speak extensively with tourist-shoppers while I helped them select merchandise. In the course of research I met many tourists who first visited San Lorenzo 10, 20, even 30 or more years ago. Like some of my students, they had made a point of returning. They happily shared memories of earlier shopping experiences. A former Delta airline stewardess described her initial visit in 1987. She laughed when she told me, "We thought we had died and gone to heaven. We bought white leather boots and jackets!" A Canadian man who last visited in 1983 remarked,

> I remember this place as a lot noisier. People shouted to one another, not vendors shouting at tourists like you hear now, but vendors calling to other vendors. You knew that these guys were here for the duration. You felt like you were walking into a family. It really seemed like one big family of vendors. There were more generations here. Looks to me like more than one generation at a stand is an anomaly these days. Sad to see! This place used to have a lot more Italians and a lot fewer stands. Maybe I'm wrong, but I don't remember any stands even being *on* this street. Almost no one spoke English back then. I think it feels different now. Don't get me wrong, it's a good market. But I wouldn't say that it is the *same* market it used to be. [his emphasis].

North American visitors usually responded very positively to learning that I was from the United States. Dozens of conversations followed from someone's realization that they were being served by an American, and some of those conversations evolved into very valuable interviews. Listening to accounts of visitors' marketplace expeditions led me to recognize the strong desire on the part of many to have what some described as a "real Italian experience." It was in the course of those interviews that I discovered their preference for frequenting Italian vendors (Schiller 2008).

A visitor from New Jersey told me, "You know, I can buy all this stuff cheaper at home. You know T.J. Maxx, right? All the same stuff! They buy it wholesale and send it to Newark in a freighter. But I want to buy it where it comes from. Italian stuff from an Italian. That [experience] means more to me than money." A shopper from Toronto explained that she preferred doing business with Italian merchants because of their comportment, noting, "It is just wonderful to buy things from Italians. I have been really uncomfortable at some of the stalls where I feel like I am being pushed to buy. But Italian vendors are lovely. This is part of the whole experience of being in Florence, a lovely Italian vendor who sells artwork versus someone from who knows where who sells sunglasses off a box. With an Italian, it's authentic. They talk to each other in Italian, and I appreciate it when somebody offers a kind word to me, a tourist. Not just yell 'Discount! Discount!'" A Californian made a similar comment: "It is different when you buy from an Italian. Italians want to relate to you, not just to sell you something. Other people just sell stuff, but the Italians want to relate to you as a person. This lady here [indicating a member of the family for whom I worked] cares about what she sells; she wants you to know that you are buying something lovely. Lots of [non-Italian] merchants are nice, but the transactions feel more commercial. I want to buy from an Italian."

Some international tourist-shoppers recognize that they do not actually possess the ability to distinguish native-born Italian vendors from individuals whom they think "look Italian," or from someone who is simply able to speak Italian. One woman, whose strategy in this regard was not unique, explained the extra step she takes to ensure that she buys from an Italian vendor. She explained, "I ask, 'where are you from?' again and again, and it goes on and on. I really liked a leather jacket, and I asked the vendor where he was from. He took a long time but he finally said, 'I have an Italian passport.' Turns out he was born in Kuwait and holds an Italian, Kuwaiti, German, and one other passport. I didn't buy the jacket. It was the same with a ceramics dealer. You have to be careful when you shop. Just keep asking!"

The fact that some tourist-shoppers prefer to buy from Italians places obvious strain on non-Italian and naturalized merchants. I observed one immigrant vendor respond sharply to a middle-aged American male who repeatedly inquired about his country of origin. "I tell you, and then what? You won't buy from me. Why do you suppose that not everybody wants to tell you where they are from? Anyway, not all Americans tell the truth either—they say they are Canadians! There are Americans all over this market walking around with Canadian flags on their knapsacks because they are scared of terrorists!" Another non-Italian merchant admitted making untruthful statements about his origins to customers as a last resort. He admitted, "People come up to me all the time and ask if I am Italian. What difference should it make if I am Italian? If I say that I am Iranian, they just walk off. If I say that I am Iranian to Americans, they just shrivel up and hurry away. So, finally, now I tell people that I am from Sicily. At least I can get away with it, and it doesn't hurt anyone. I have to do it to make sales. If they ask me and they have already paid, I tell them I am Persian."

To recap, some tourists, in particular some North Americans, come to San Lorenzo Market at least partly in search of opportunities to interact with Italians in what they consider to be an authentic setting. They also believe that purchasing items from Italian vendors is what makes their shopping experience in San Lorenzo authentic. The next section begins to probe attitudes of some *sanlorenzini* on similar matters of authenticity, identity, and heritage.

Identity and Heritage in a World Heritage Site

Sanlorenzini encounter people from across the globe as well as from across the street at this neighborhood market every day. Over time the market has become physically larger, more heavily touristed, and more socially diverse. That diversity was explicitly recognized in the theme of the 2007 celebration of the patron saint's day: "San Lorenzo: A Thousand Worlds in One Place." When Florentines say they are going to this market, they state simply, "*Io vo a San Lorenzo*," revealing that the neighborhood is identified with the market as well as the other way around. Though they continue to talk about it a great deal, fewer are actually shopping there. Asked why, the most common responses are that it has changed, lost its identity, lost its *fiorentinità*, or for various reasons, usually linked somehow to globalization, is less appealing than before. People sometimes suggest that the market's fate is iconic of the entire city, of Italy, or even of Europe itself. There are some who agree with the Italian journalist Oriana Fallaci's claim that the notions of "Florentine," "Italian," and "merchant," and even European heritage itself are at risk (Fallaci 2002).[10]

---

10 Oriana Fallaci (1929–2006) was a Florentine author and social critic who originally earned her international reputation as a war correspondent. Among the best known of her later works was her 2001 book *The Rage and the Pride*, written in the immediate aftermath of the September 11, 2001, terrorist attacks on the United States. Fallaci's forcefully anti-immigration stance in that volume, published in English in 2002, and subsequent work won admiration in some quarters and criticism in others. In Florence, whether and how to recognize Fallaci's legacy led to rancorous debate between political groups (Mazzoni 2006).

Many *sanlorenzini* consider some consequences of globalization in this market to be problematic. For example, one of my student research assistants asked a Central Market fishmonger what he considered the most difficult aspects of his job. "Waking up early to buy fish," he laughed, "and pigeons getting inside past the doors!" The student and I later began meeting occasionally with this vendor and patronizing his business. In the course of a conversation several visits later, he nodded at the enormous poster of a violet lily symbolizing the Fiorentina soccer team taped to his wall and said, "It is hard to keep my heritage in this place." That remark opened the way for me to pursue a more extensive interview about heritage and diversity. It was clear that for him, and for others, working in San Lorenzo or shopping there today is a qualitatively different experience than it was 30 years ago. The change is usually attributed to the effects of migration and tourism.

In the years since the historic center of Florence, which includes San Lorenzo, was officially declared a UNESCO World Heritage Site, heritage and identity issues have become even more complicated in this neighborhood. While it was once the "Pulse Point of Florentine Life," many in this city today find San Lorenzo difficult to characterize. Is it Florentine, or is it something else? Does it preserve heritage or undermine it? Such questions regularly come up in conversation that surrounds daily life.

Heritage is also a topic that now receives a great deal of attention across academic disciplines and from professionals in the field (Breathnach 2006: 16; Macdonald 1993: 65; Throsby 2003). At the most general level it has been described as "everything that people want to save" (Howard 2003: 1), but its definition continues to evolve. For example, in the 1960s and 1970s the term was used mostly to refer to tangible assets such as monuments, buildings, and similar features (Ahmad 2006). It is obvious, of course, that many vendors capitalize on the city's extraordinary artistic heritage. Perhaps some readers of this book have already visited Florence and had the experience of going to the Accademia Gallery to view Michelangelo's statue of David, and then walked around the corner to the San Lorenzo Market and found hundreds of reproductions of that statue for sale. There is a seemingly infinite selection of depictions of Florence's material heritage reproduced on magnets, shot glasses, spoon rests, commemorative plates, laser-cut paperweights, thimbles, key chains, cigarette lighters, calendars, bottle openers, snow globes, ashtrays, pens, hand fans, pill boxes, postcards, miniature bells, jacket patches, pencils, rulers, pins, tee-shirts, aprons, and even underwear.

Heritage is not restricted, however, to the masterful objects or buildings that distinguish grand cities. It also refers to the natural environment as well as cultural and social phenomena. Immaterial or intangible heritage, according to the UNESCO 2002 Convention for the Safeguarding of Intangible Cultural Heritage, refers to "the practices, representations, expressions, knowledge, skills—as well as the instruments, objects, artifacts and cultural spaces associated therewith—that communities, groups and, in some cases, individuals recognize as part of their cultural heritage, e.g., spiritual practices, folklore, song, dance, cuisine, to name just a few" (Samuels 2014). In that regard, Christina Kreps has made the important point that material items also encompass an immaterial heritage dimension as they communicate and transmit ideas within the context of larger social structures and social practices (2005: 4).

Conversations about heritage in San Lorenzo reveal a paradox. Niccolò, for example, remarked that he migrated there for reasons only partly having to do with earning a living. He could have gone elsewhere, but Florence makes him feel "inspired." On the one hand, many vendors are proud to work surrounded by buildings and art with strong heritage associations and to offer merchandise commemorating heritage. Some of my informants, in fact, would rather be known as "historic vendors" than "ambulant vendors," to emphasize the link between the San Lorenzo Market and the story of this city. On the other hand, it is obvious that fewer native-born Florentines are seeking work in San Lorenzo or even shopping there. Many claim that they avoid San Lorenzo altogether because, in their opinion, the marketplace has lost its *fiorentinità*, and because they have no interest in much of the available wares.

How is it that San Lorenzo can be considered both heritage rich and heritage poor at the same time? Clues are found in the notion of *fiorentinità*. The recent renovation of the Central Market provides an example. The refurbishment of the building's first floor and replacement of the dumpsters behind it with underground trash receptacles are part of efforts to preserve material heritage and improve quality of life. But according to many vendors, the serpentine arcade for greengrocers that stood behind the building until 1976 was also an important piece of heritage. The empty space where the portico once stood signifies, to them, lost *fiorentinità*. Despite the long, costly, and handsome renovation of the market building's first floor, the portico was not replaced. Not rebuilding the portico signifies that the number of greengrocers able to work there will be significantly and permanently reduced, which vendors say is a further loss of *fiorentinità*. Still, it is obvious that even some *sanlorenzini* no longer rely on these providers. Over the past decade, in a situation that is certainly not unique to Florence, supermarkets with extended hours of operation have become popular among many urban residents (Counihan 2004: 128). Large chain stores with ample parking, as well as big-box stores, are found just outside the city center. More to the point, the number of small supermarkets within the historic district is increasing steadily, and a medium-sized supermarket has opened directly across the street from the San Lorenzo Church. When I commenced this project there was just one supermarket located within a 10-minute walk of the Central Market. Now there are at least seven of various sizes. In addition, the neighborhood incorporates several specialty grocery stores that primarily sell Asian or Latin American foods. Four "99 Cent" stores, which carry pasta, some canned goods, kitchen items, cleaning supplies, and even inexpensive souvenirs, have also opened, including two just a few hundred meters from market *banchi*.

It thus becomes clear that many who claim that heritage is at risk in San Lorenzo are referring to something in addition to disappearing arcades. They are expressing nostalgia for kinds of work, modes of interacting, and sounds and sights that are not as common as before. Yet at the same time, reducing the number of vendors operating in this zone is considered by many civic authorities and even some San Lorenzo stakeholders as one way to restore San Lorenzo's *fiorentinità* rather than diminish it. Later chapters address in more detail this apparent incongruity and its consequences.

The next chapter shifts focus from San Lorenzo's past to its present, in particular to the experiences of the marketplace vendors among whom my students and I conducted research. Among those whose activities are highlighted are members of a merchant family with whom I have apprenticed for a decade. The chapter describes vendors' day-to-day activities, including coping with the weather, operating a *banco* or finding work at one, interacting with clients, competitors and friends, and confronting old and new challenges in a socially fluid environment. It shows that globalization has directly affected vendors in ways that implicate how they make a living, how they construct and express their identity, and how their work life comports with notions of *fiorentinità*.

CHAPTER THREE

LIVES AND LIVELIHOODS ON SILVER STREET

"Sheep in the sky, water in buckets," Signora Ivana Beati-Blandae remarked dispiritedly as she watched dark clouds gathering overhead one chilly November morning. Portents of rain meant fewer shoppers. The month was notorious for slow sales. Business revived as the holidays approached, but December was still far off. In the previous two hours, Ivana had managed only three sales: a palm-sized reproduction of Michelangelo's David, a shot glass decorated with a sketch of the cathedral, and an aluminum cigarette lighter bearing the likeness of the late pope, Saint John Paul II. There were just seven and a half euros in the cash box, 22 per cent of it to be paid in taxes. Signor Silvio, Ivana's husband, rubbed his hands together against the cold and sighed, "Here we have a misery you can cut with a knife."

Not long afterward, the skies unleashed a chilly torrent on shoppers, merchants, and merchandise. All along Silver Street, which takes its name from the activities of silver workers who manufactured silver thread there 500 years ago, vendors scrambled to protect their *banchi*. A sudden burst of wind and they redoubled efforts to secure canvas awnings and prevent merchandise from blowing away. "What a squall!," Ivana cried out, as she wrestled plastic sheeting over a display of gilt-framed Florence cityscapes. A Pinocchio marionette, blown loose from a hook, abruptly dived into a puddle of water and snapped off his nose. Resin angels, suspended on invisible threads, thrashed and twisted. Eva, who works directly across from the Beati-Blandae family, whipped out a tarpaulin to protect her scarves and ties. She was having trouble attaching the heavy canvas to the roof of her *banco* with one hand while gripping a rickety ladder with the other. Ivana's son, Dante, dashed to her aid. "I hate wind," Eva called out as she brushed raindrops from her face. "Rain is bad, but wind is worse." The crash of hand-painted ceramic pitchers toppling from someone else's *banco* cut her short. Shoppers scurried for cover in doorways. Deliverymen sped past on bicycles, heads down against the wind. Yet not everyone was put off by the bad weather. As quickly as the storm had arrived, so too had a group of unlicensed entrepreneurs toting armfuls of €5 umbrellas, hoping to find a silver lining in the clouds letting loose on Silver Street.

Coping with weather, managing inventory, interacting with customers, keeping an eye on associates and rivals—these are all typical activities in a vendor's day. No one knows whether the day will end with €500 in the cash box, or 50, or 15. Yet the merchants of San Lorenzo derive a satisfaction that many people might envy from how they make a living. This chapter offers a snapshot of their work lives, a portrait of the ordinary. It focuses on the activities of a multigenerational family of Florentine vendors and their marketplace neighbors. It explores how these and other vendors got their start, how they manage their time and resources, and what they consider to be some important non-monetary rewards of their occupation. The latter include the satisfaction they derive from participating in what they hope to be long-lasting relationships with clients and other merchants, their professional autonomy, and the pride they feel in being associated with this historic marketplace.

How Some Vendors Got Their Start

"Beautiful stuff, ladies and gentlemen," Silvio Beati-Blandae murmurs as passersby cast fleeting looks at his *banco*. Well into his eighties, Silvio still cuts a charming and vigorous figure in the tweed cap and layered shirts with which he confronts daylong stints in biting cold. "Ladies and gentlemen, we are at your service," Silvio says to no one in particular. His gentle enticements fail to garner much interest at that moment. He shrugs and pokes out his bottom lip in resignation.

Silvio has over 50 years of experience as an outdoor vendor. He says he began even earlier because he passed his infancy at a market stand. His mother, Belinda, owned a New Market *banco* that she inherited when her own mother died in the 1919 Spanish influenza epidemic. After nursing her infant son, Belinda would put him down to nap in a *banco* drawer and turn her attention back to selling straw hats.

As a young man, Silvio fought in World War II, spent time as a prisoner of war, and endured other hardships associated with wartime Italy. He met his future wife, Ivana, years later while auditioning dancers for his father's touring vaudeville troupe. Silvio eventually followed in his mother's footsteps, although he did not take up vending full time until he had a child of his own. When their son Dante was born, Ivana gave up dancing, and the couple joined Belinda and other relatives at the New Market. When Belinda died, Silvio's older brother became proprietor of her *banco*. Silvio used his inheritance, which included a vending license, to set up a *banco* in

San Lorenzo, where the merchandise that he intended to sell would be less commonplace. Silvio and Ivana christened their new *banco* "Belinda 63" in memory of his mother, whose *banco* had been located at New Market niche 63. Silvio and Ivana have now maintained a presence in San Lorenzo for four decades. Their family, which operates one of the longest-lived enterprises in the outdoor market, is recognized for the good relations that they cultivate with fellow vendors and admired for the quality of their merchandise. They are exemplary vendors.

As when Silvio and Ivana worked at his mother's *banco* in the New Market, two generations of family members work side by side in San Lorenzo. Dante, who is now the registered owner of the *banco*, became full-time after graduating from high school. Beatrice, his wife, joined full time when their daughter Azzurra entered primary school. Dante and Beatrice jointly decide what merchandise to carry. Beatrice sets prices and manages relations with wholesalers and artisans. Dante, who has a gift for design, is the authority on how to display the stock. Occasionally Dante's own artwork can be found on sale there, too.

Silvio and Ivana are among the handful of senior vendors who continue to put in entire days at the market. Entrepreneurial spirit, a desire to connect with others, and habit propel these old hands to show up each morning, even on days when relatives, friends, and the national weather service urge older adults to stay indoors. Their only concessions to age are to leave the arduous task of unpacking merchandise to others and to take a taxi home in the evening. Long hours standing in the market exacerbate Ivana's arthritis, a widespread malady among vendors who spend decades standing outdoors in every type of weather.

For elderly vendors, passing their license and *banco* to their children is a first choice. A second choice is selling or renting the business to another entrepreneur. A vending license can be a valuable inheritance. Depending upon the economy and one's location, a license and *banco* in San Lorenzo can be worth up to €200,000 exclusive of merchandise. The fact that a *banco* or shop has been passed down through multiple generations can be a source of pride. But today fewer children seem to want the responsibilities of operating a *banco*. When the children of one family decided to sell their family's business inside the Central Market, for example, they left a handwritten sign taped high up on the wall behind the counter, underlined for emphasis:

AFTER 99 YEARS

THE PREMIER CHICKEN BUTCHER

"GIOVANNI"

TERMINATES ACTIVITY

THE FAMILY THANKS ITS GRACIOUS CLIENTELE.

The fact that children who stand to inherit their family's operation are choosing to pursue different careers is a situation affecting family enterprises in Italy generally (Corbetta 1995).[1] While Dante chose to continue his parents' business, neither his daughter Azzurra nor her husband, Mik, intend to take over the Silver Street *banco*. They secured state jobs. Azzurra frequently stops by with her infant son to visit her parents and grandparents, but she does not interact with customers.

Inheriting a license or marrying into a market family was, until recently, a way in which many vendors got their start. George the bread man, who operates a *banco* on the Central Market's ground floor with his younger brother Evan, is another example. While in his early 20s, George earned a diploma in tourism services management. The positions he held following graduation, however, offered little opportunity for advancement. So while George initially resisted his father's invitation to take over the business, he and his brother eventually changed their minds. They could often be spotted pulling their truck up to a bakery across town at 4:00 in the morning, six days a week, to buy bread for resale in San Lorenzo.

Other paths bring other vendors to the market. Carlo, who specializes in high-end balsamic vinegars, wine, cheeses, and cured sausages, used to make costume jewelry. He sold earrings outside the train station in the 1980s. Over time he was able to afford to move to the open-air market. He diversified and bought an oil and wine shop inside the Central Market building. Together with his wife Sinta, whom he met during a vacation abroad, Carlo expanded his interests to include two additional Central Market shops, part of a grocery store located behind the San Lorenzo Church, and an olive oil shop on one of the city's most prestigious streets, near the famous *Ponte Vecchio* that spans the Arno River. GianLuca came to San Lorenzo under very different circumstances. He decided to join his companion Alessandra at her clothing *banco* after his graduate studies at the Massachusetts Institute of Technology. Because he once lived in the United States, fellow vendors turn to him for predictions about how the US economy may affect their businesses. Niccolò, the purse vendor from Basilicata, like GianLuca, came to San Lorenzo after university study; he had moved to the city three decades ago to study biology at the University of Florence. Among the residents of his boarding house at the time was Akka, originally from Iran. Akka and Niccolò became friends and launched a partnership selling quality leather briefcases and purses on Silver Street nearly 20 years ago. Their collaboration is the longest-lasting non-family joint enterprise in San Lorenzo.

---

1 Corbetta refers to this phenomenon as "the cooling off of family partners." He states, "The founder(s) identify completely with the business they began…. With the passing of generations it is natural for these affective or affinity ties to slacken; the strong identification with the business weakens" (1995: 259).

Although they came by very different paths, Akka and Niccolò are both migrants to Florence and San Lorenzo. Kevin and his younger brother Cristoforo, whose thoughts about seeing the world from San Lorenzo were quoted in Chapter Two, have similarly been in San Lorenzo for a very long time, having left Iran shortly before the Shah fell from power. They initially rented a *banco* behind the Central Market where, like many Middle Eastern immigrants, they specialized in leather jackets. In time they amassed enough money to rent and then purchase a leather shop within sight of the Central Market's front doors. Word of mouth and excellent reviews on the Internet bring many North American customers their way. Although they do not employ sales assistants, they allowed one of my student research assistants to work as a volunteer in their shop. Her research focused on the acculturative strategies of immigrant entrepreneurs, and she presented her findings at a major professional meeting for anthropologists (Schiller and Gordon 2007).

Eva, who sells scarves and ties, arrived 10 years ago after resigning her corporate position in Argentina as a mid-level manager for a US-based fast-food restaurant chain. After she became disillusioned with American politics, she left her job and pooled resources with a group of compatriots to purchase a hotel in Florence. When she moved there she began working part time for a scarf merchant and discovered that retail work, and greater autonomy, suited her. She sold her interest in the hotel and signed a multi-year lease on a *banco*. Eva occasionally hires other Latin American women to work for her, and she also accepted one of my student researchers as a volunteer. That student's project focused on merchants' life histories. Her findings were presented in an article she co-authored and published with the student researcher who conducted fieldwork in Kevin and Christopher's shop (Gordon and Shunmugamm 2007).

Eva is one of a very few independent female entrepreneurs who run a *banco* in San Lorenzo, and one of an even smaller group of foreign women who do so. While the vendors I have just mentioned all arrived at least a decade ago, there is now a large number of new immigrant vendors in San Lorenzo. Some are expatriates from poor countries or occupied territories. Some come only for a season for particular work. Some recent immigrants are day laborers who arrive routinely after dawn each day hoping that an owner will need them at that time or will be impressed and offer them regular work.

Merchants and Their Merchandise

Sanlorenzini often say that "the one who sleeps doesn't catch fish," similar to the proverb "the early bird catches the worm." Vendors start their workday early, many long before sunrise. By 5:30 a.m., for example, George and Evan have completed their transaction at the wholesale bakery, filled their truck with warm bread, and are on their way back to the historic center. Jacopo has finished his daily trek to buy fruit and vegetables at the wholesale market on the city outskirts and is driving back as well. Just before 6:00 a.m., they can all be spotted among the crowd of merchants assembled on the Central Market steps waiting for the police to open the doors. Two hours later, the public is allowed to enter. Ground-floor vendors have little flexibility in their hours because their shops are required to close at 2:00 p.m. sharp. Saturday is the only day when ground-floor vendors are permitted to operate longer, until 5:00 p.m. On Sundays and national holidays, ground-floor businesses must remain closed. First-floor operations are open to the public seven days a week until late in the evening.

Open-air vendors begin selling later in the morning, but they, too, must start their preparations early. An outdoor vendor's first morning task is to extract his or her *banco* from storage and wheel it to its allotted space. The clatter of wooden wheels bumping across paving stones at daybreak is one of San Lorenzo's characteristic noises. *Banchi* are kept in cavernous ground-floor garages located in dozens of nearby buildings, where space can be rented monthly for €500. When Dante and Beatrice arrive at the market, however, their *banco* is already out of the garage. Like others who can afford it, they contract with a porter service that stows and unstows their *banco* for €100 per week. The work is usually performed by immigrant laborers. Porters retrieve *banchi* and roll them back to the garage by 7:30 p.m. on winter evenings and 8:30 p.m. in the summer. That schedule is firm, because each cart must be removed before street cleaners arrive for the zone's nightly scrub-down.

Once a *banco* has reached its assigned space in the morning, it must be readied for business. Some marketers employ men and women, again, mostly immigrant day laborers, to perform this work, which is aptly called "open/ close." For set-up, side panels are removed; tarps are raised in anticipation of sun, rain, or snow; drawers are opened so that they can be filled with merchandise; and any merchandise left in the *banco* from the previous day is arranged for display. Among the immigrant workers is "Michelangelo," who came from Romania in 2005 and has opened and closed *banchi* since the day he arrived in this city. He got his local moniker from his first Florentine employer, who was impressed by the imaginative way he arranged merchandise. "I like the name Michelangelo," he told me. "It reflects the quality of my work and suits the life I am making for myself in Florence." He added with a smile, "When I start my own business I am going to print business cards that say 'Michelangelo of Florence.' How is that for marketing?!" He continued,

> I have a first class honors degree in engineering from my country. I had to leave Romania because of a business scandal in which my boss tried to implicate me. Of course, at the time I immigrated I was without papers

FIGURE 3.1: Silver Street *banchi* waiting to be re-garaged overnight.
CREDIT: Anne Schiller

and could not have applied for work as an engineer in Italy.[2] I had no other work, just this. I would stand here all day, even though the owner only needed me for two hours. It was just in case I could run an errand or if some part of the *banco* broke. Then I could pick up a little extra money. It went on like this for a few years. Now I work here for two hours on my way to and from other jobs; I do a lot of home remodeling for rich Florentines.

Michelangelo receives €20 a day, paid in cash at the end of the week, for his work at the *banco*. If pressed for time or simply trying to help out a fellow Romanian immigrant, he lets people assist him. As his home remodeling jobs increase, he relies more on compatriot "subcontractors." The practice of sharing work is not unusual in the informal sector. With an employer's permission, day laborers often find their own replacements on a temporary or permanent basis.

When Silvio, Ivana, Dante, and Beatrice convene each morning, the older couple attends to clients while the younger one finishes unpacking

---

2 Michelangelo came to Italy as an irregular immigrant, although he is now legally permitted to work there. For more on recent Romanian immigration to Italy, see Tragaki and Rovolis (2014).

and arranging merchandise. Like most open-air vendors, Dante and Beatrice warehouse their merchandise in a nearby set of rented rooms in an apartment building across the street from their *banco*. The monthly fee for the space is €550. At the beginning of each day, they trundle back and forth between their *banco* and their "warehouse," procuring merchandise. By 9:00 a.m., their *banco* is fully loaded. From that moment through to the close of business, they rarely venture more than a few feet away, except to take turns having a sandwich or coffee or a trip to the warehouse to replenish their stock. On Fridays, Dante and some other male vendors may take a longer lunch, where they chat about the victories or losses of their beloved soccer team, Fiorentina. Still, they seldom frequent restaurants that are more than a two- or three-minute walk from their businesses. At the end of each day they engage in the same activities associated with setting up, but in reverse order.

Vendors call the daily cost of doing business in San Lorenzo the *giornata*. Warehouse space, fees for porter service, and paying someone to open and close are not the only expenses. Some merchants hook up electricity to have lights in their *banco*, run a heater or a fan, or operate a credit-card machine. Some have a land-line phone. Their biggest business-related expense, however, aside from securing a license or continuously buying merchandise, is the annual fee paid to the city for the right to use "public space." Fees for the use of public space grant vendors use of a delineated area of the pavement

FIGURE 3.2: Vendors gather behind a *banco* to watch a televised soccer match.
CREDIT: Anne Schiller

outside or a space inside the Central Market. Fees are set by the City Council and vary by location.[3] The "San Lorenzo Cluster," like the New Market across town, is considered a "Category One" market, for which fees are highest. In 2010, the City Council nearly doubled the fee. As a result, Dante and Beatrice, like their outdoor neighbors, now pay €9,000 annually (over US$10,000) for the right to occupy a two-by-three-meter patch of asphalt during daylight hours.

Many factors affect net earnings, including the popularity of the merchandise, the number of hours worked, location within the market, the weather, the season, what the competition is doing, local and international economies, talent, and luck. Some days are obviously better than others in this type of work environment. When factors conjoin to produce a not-so-good day, marketers may lament, "We are cadavers," or "We are on our deathbeds today." I recall one stifling June afternoon when my student assistants and I were seated on the steps of the Central Market building going over our field journals. We noticed smoke plumes wafting from a nearby *banco* stocked with souvenirs. The sun's rays, passing though snow globes, had ignited the boxes behind them. The frustrated vendor slapped at the smoldering cardboard with a towel and shouted, "Seven wretched hours, 35 pitiful euro! Not even the *giornata* today and now a fire."

His situation makes clear that earning a living in San Lorenzo requires a steady presence. Like the Beati-Blandae family, the majority of vendors work six days a week. Some keep even more arduous schedules. Mansour, who came to Florence 20 years ago from Iran, grants himself one day off every two weeks. Sishir, a Bangladeshi who sells silver jewelry, can afford only one free day each month right now. Still, although many struggle, a skillful vendor who carries popular merchandise in a visible location can net €40,000–60,000 annually. A few are rumored to take home six figures.

Finding Work in San Lorenzo

Business owners are not the only people whom shoppers may encounter at a *banco*. Some vendors hire sales assistants, some of whom have been in the market a long time. Franco has been selling clothing from the same spot on Millet Street for 13 years. His Florentine boss works alongside him but, as he said with a hint of pride, "I do alright for the two of us. I speak English and she is quiet. Maybe it's because I am younger. Maybe it's because I'm Roman that I am successful! She watches me work all day and here I am,

---

3 Detailed information regarding the Tax for Occupation of Spaces and Public Areas (COSAP) is posted at: http://servizi.comune.fi.it/scheda-servizio/canone-occupazione-spazi-ed-aree-pubbliche

even after all these years." Other assistants follow the seasons, working there some months and then moving elsewhere. One such worker from Morocco explained, "It isn't easy, but I can find work here in May, when tourists start coming. I go to France for work in October. There won't be much for me in Florence then." An irregular immigrant from Eastern Europe who had worked for his current boss for six months commented, "I have to be sure not to make problems for the boss. If I don't keep good relations with people at the other *banchi*, they might raise questions about [my immigration status] or about my boss [hiring me]. It is hard working outside, sure, but I need work. I worked at two leather stands before this one, and my wages were pitiful. Thirty euro a day, cash. My last bosses let me go when things got slack; that would be October. That will probably happen to me this year, too. If I stay here, I can also pick up seasonal work for a few weeks in December." A North American who had overstayed her tourist visa because she wanted to live in Florence, thus joining the ranks of the other irregular immigrants, told me:

> It is a little humiliating trying to get work; I just go from *banco* to *banco* asking if they need someone. It's hard and you have to be persistent. Anyway, right now I am working 10-hour days, about average here, and earn four euro an hour. Some of us work on commission. When I started here, my boss told me how far down I could go if someone asked for a discount. After a while, you get a sense of what a customer will pay. I can just make up a number and not be far off. I can go way down on a leather jacket, but lambskin, never below 200 euro. The price you offer depends on whether you are on commission.

A Latin American described her experience searching for a job inside the Central Market:

> It was hard to find a job because business is slow, but I can speak some English so I just went to a few places and asked if they needed someone who could speak other languages. I kept coming back, asking if there was work. Finally, a job! 7 a.m. to 3 p.m., six days, 40 euro a day. Not bad. My boss is kind to me as far as they go, because if I get sick she will still put half a day's pay in my envelope. Sometimes she brings coffee, a pastry, or even a sandwich. I used to say that I didn't want the sandwich. I was afraid that she would think I was the type to take advantage. Now I take it because, at four euro a sandwich, that is an hour of work for me!

Asked to describe her job, she emphasized she was always busy:

> Believe me, there is no such thing as a break. I rarely see anyone sit down, and standing all day is hard on the back. I wash and mop floors, clean

cutting boards and knives, dust stock, and put food out. I sometimes stand out front and greet people. That lets me practice my English, and the owner wants it. Other employees are jealous because I am out front while they clean. But I know English, some French, Spanish obviously. Everyone is afraid they will lose their jobs. I don't want anyone to lose their job, but I sure hope they keep me when the tourists slow down.

Some vendors say that they take on temporary staff as a favor to those down on their luck. They do not feel compelled to report to the tax office the names of those for whom they are doing this good deed, which would also require them to make pension contributions. They characterize it as trial employment to see if a worker is worth keeping. When I asked one vendor why he dismissed someone after only two weeks, he shrugged and replied with a humorous ditty: "Desire to work, jump on top of me, and [then] make me work as little as possible." In other words, the fellow interviewed well but turned out to be lazy in his employer's opinion.

Competition in Close Quarters

Many outdoor vendors specialize in the sale of artisanal crafts. Florentine artisanal goods in San Lorenzo include handmade papers, an array of leather items, distinctive local ceramics, and gilded hand-painted traditional trays. Artisanal work on sale from outside Tuscany includes Murano glass ornaments, Venetian masks, and wooden and horn carvings from Africa. Some vendors sell merchandise that is entirely "Made in Italy." Others sell merchandise made of imported materials and simply finished in Italy. Some sell novelty items imported from Asia. Dante and Beatrice specialize in Florentine artisanal crafts. Their suppliers include some men in their eighties with whom the family has dealt since Dante's grandmother's days at the New Market.

Regardless of what is sold, all vendors must develop their understanding of the product and identify wholesalers, distributors, or artisans with whom they can work. Not everyone specializes in their favorite goods. Eva, for example, would rather stock vintage clothing than scarves and ties. She says that used clothing appeals more to the working-class city residents to whom she would rather sell than to tourists. That there are currently no other used-clothing vendors on Silver Street encourages her, but she points out that many locals, her preferred target, avoid the market because they say it caters to tourists. Eva believes there would not be enough of a local clientele to support the switch and it would be too much of a gamble.

If Eva did make the shift, she could do so without making a formal request to the city government, or even consulting with a neighbor who may be selling the same thing. There are few restrictions about what a vendor can sell outdoors, as long as it is legal and not food. But vendors' options were not always so flexible. In years past the city regulated the minimum distance that had to be maintained between two outside businesses offering the same type of merchandise. In those days, vendors registered a list of goods they carried with the city's commercial office, which performed spot checks to confirm that the vendors were selling only what they promised. Although merchants today continue to record lists with the authorities of the merchandise carried, restrictions concerning merchandise type and distance between vendors were lifted in the early 1990s.

The abolishment of "redundancy rules" was helpful, some merchants argue, because vendors can now respond quickly to consumers' changing tastes and budgets. At the same time, most agree that relations among vendors have become more difficult as a result. For example, a survey conducted by my student assistants in 2008 revealed that of 59 *banchi* that operated in a two-block section of Silver Street, 9 dealt in scarves and/or ties, 9 in leather purses or wallets, and 8 in artisanal crafts. Redundancy was also apparent, to a lesser degree, in the remaining 33 *banchi*. In 2013, the same area included roughly equivalent numbers of enterprises offering scarves/ties and artisanal work. The number of *banchi* offering purses and wallets (some of these also offered jackets, but the bulk of the merchandise was purses or wallets), however, had ballooned to 36. One exasperated merchant, who had just arrived at the market to find that the owner of the cart beside his had begun to offer handmade leather photo albums nearly identical to the ones that he had been carrying for years, groused, "One of the biggest problems is that we all sell the same thing. Big diversity in people, but hardly anybody carries something different. A few years ago, all scarves. Not just scarves but the same scarves. Down Millet Street, nothing but leather. Iranians and Chinese all selling jackets that were identical except for the label. The City Council should do something about this problem. We can't go back in time, but we can't go forward this way, either." As his predicament illustrates, a vendor cannot know whether a neighbor will suddenly decide to carry merchandise like his own. One's livelihood is put at risk quickly if a competitor offering similar goods has even a seemingly small advantage such as a location closer to a lively intersection or better wholesale prices.

Given the high levels of redundancy, open-market enterprises seem very alike at first glance. Upon closer inspection, however, their differences are more evident. For example, how vendors present their merchandise to the public is testament to their artistic sensibilities as well as business acumen. Some say that a *banco*, like a person, should "make a good impression." Rarely is any aspect of its appearance left unconsidered, as I learned when a vendor called me over to discuss his new display. I told him I thought it looked lovely but that he might consider covering the labels on the shoeboxes on which snow globes were arranged. "But these are Gucci boxes!" he replied with dismay, "They set a tone!"

While all vendors display merchandise with care, no one way is typical. A *banco* specializing in woolen caps may be organized by colors, looking like a rainbow one day and a checkerboard the next. The owner of a leather cart may hang jackets in particular cuts symmetrically to frame the open spot where he or she stands waiting for customers, while his competitor uses mannequins that resemble popular movie stars to model jackets. Some merchants abhor open spaces. Others leave space around each item to high-light its particularities. The cart itself, too, may be decorated and made more eye-catching. One ambitious vendor stenciled enormous red lilies, symbols of the city, on the sides of his *banco*. Passersby often stopped to photograph it, and then began sorting through his merchandise.

Ennio, who deals in artisanal Florentine wooden trays, is pleased when he overhears customers talking about his attractive *banco*. "Why not?" he said. "This is the city of art. I do not paint, I do not sculpt, but I am sur-rounded by the beauty of Florence. Therefore, I try to bring beauty to my *banco*. My *banco* is my canvas." Ennio, like his counterparts, tempers aesthet-ics with entrepreneurial instinct. Some vendors prefer to arrange objects by relative price, from least to most expensive. Potential clients may be drawn initially to an inexpensive item near the front, and then spot something more appealing and pricier farther back. Rotating stock in hopes of catching the right buyer's eye is common. Merchants engage in a seemingly endless cycle of rearranging, reorganizing, and refolding, making countless minute adjustments throughout the day. A decorated saucer is exhibited on a tiny tripod between two shot glasses to make it more noticeable. Two hours later, the saucer has been moved to the side of a resin reproduction of Cellini's sculpture "Perseus with the Head of Medusa." A particular piece of merchan-dise may disappear for months, tucked away on a shelf in the warehouse, and then make a sudden reappearance. Vendors continually strategize about where to place particular pieces of merchandise within their extremely limited confines. They must be careful not to take up even a few centimeters more than their allotted space, as law-enforcement officers from the Ministry of Finance regularly patrol the marketplace with tape measures, and merchants are fined hundreds of euros when they violate the rule.

When they are not contemplating their own *banco*, vendors cast a sur-reptitious eye at others in order to inform themselves about the state of competitors' businesses. They may also hope to glimpse the suppliers who provision their rivals. San Lorenzo vendors are not unique in this regard. In his study of peasant marketing in Morocco, for example, Clifford Geertz observed that "the search for information one lacks and the protection of information one has is the name of the game" (1978: 29). Ethnographers who have conducted fieldwork in markets elsewhere have made similar observations. In her investigations of the *as-souq* (market) in Aleppo, Syria, for instance, Annika Rabo characterizes "the whole of Aleppo as a market for information, where both demand and supply are amply available" (2005: 32). That information, Rabo points out, "is not used solely, or perhaps mainly, to further one's immediate business interests … it is also a means of expressing oneself in capacities other than money-making" (32). As one might expect, great differences exist among traders in the *souq* over "how intensely they participate in the receiving and spreading of information." But even the most quiet and restrained trader is "informed and contributes to informing others" (34).

Theodore Bestor has also commented regarding the "relational contracting" ties that bind trading partners and auctioneers in the Tsukiji district of Tokyo, that "chief among them is the flow of information" (2004: 204). Auctioneers in Tsukiji's expansive seafood market "survey miniscule domains about which they command vastly detailed information about the relevant commodities, their producers, and the preferences and purchasing patterns of traders" (207). The successful exchange of information is a two-way street, Bestor claims, with auction houses obtaining the highest average prices "only for suppliers with whom they are in frequent if not constant contact" (209).

Linda Seligmann examines every aspect of the distribution chain in her study on market women in Cuzco, Peru. In that setting, identity and language are closely linked and often provide parameters that protect the exchange of information and distribution of products (2004: 84). Information is no less important for the Maya vendors of Guatemala, according to Walter Little, who reports that many confident vendors actually encourage customers to price shop, or gather their own information, because many are often ignorant of prices elsewhere in the market. Information is thus used by vendors (and ideally customers, too) so that both sides can come to an agreement about the price of the object for sale (Little 2004: 119).

While monitoring business at competitors' *banchi* is normal in San Lorenzo, discretion is advised. Vendors suspected of eavesdropping on competitors' conversations about their business are disapprovingly characterized as having "straight ears," conjuring images of a dog surprised by noise, or "ears like satellite dishes." Clever marketers manage to glean information about other enterprises while giving little away about their own. "A hillock and a hole make a plain," merchants counsel, meaning that just as a hill will eventually collapse if punctured by too many excavations, the business of one who allows information to leak away will surely fail over time.

Vendors can certainly control specific information related to their supplies, their expenses, and their profit by choosing not to divulge it in conversation. Still their presence in the market and everyday behaviors are sources of information for others. Vendors do "read" other marketers' *banchi*, looking for subtle clues about how another's business is faring whether or not they carry the same merchandise. How they interpret those clues might influence how they manage their own business. The challenge is to interpret correctly the meaning of what is observed in order to make the right business decision. As an example, consider the case of a vendor who displays large quantities of a single type of merchandise. One might surmise that the vendor considers such a practice to be most economical as she only has to manage relations with one supplier. Or maybe the vendor is trying simply to suggest to potential customers that she has a specialty. Competitors who are looking at her display, however, may conclude that this type of merchandise must sell well, for why else would she limit herself? That could be enough to influence one of them to "carry some of this myself." Regardless of the accuracy of vendors' interpretations of what they see, we can be sure that the information they believe they have gleaned from their observation is filed away in their minds to be used in making decisions about their own *banco*. Of course, that interpretation may or may not have been correct. Similarly, while some *banchi* are chock-a-block with merchandise, others are not. Bare shelves may suggest limited flexibility in pricing to a competitor. A Spartan display, like a bursting one, may also embolden someone to carry a greater quantity of that same merchandise so as to entice customers away from the fellow who first carried it.

As they look at competitors' *banchi*, some vendors are also searching for fresh ideas about how to arrange merchandise. Reproducing someone's display is a major aggravation in these extremely close quarters, as is the duplication of wares. A scarf merchant grumbled, "Every time I find a new way to display my stock, that woman three stands away copies me. What a ball ... she is always watching my *banco*![4] But what can I do? I have no choice but to try to come up with something. Because of her, every morning I have to find a new way to fold scarves. My display must be unique!" One marketer who also lamented someone taking his creative ideas was Signor Roberto, known in San Lorenzo as the creator of the "*Ciao Bella*" ("Hello/Goodbye Beautiful") tee-shirt now sold widely throughout Italy. He explained:

> *Beh*, the worst mistake of my life was not copyrighting the design for that tee-shirt before I sold it. I had no idea what a huge success it would be or that someone would steal my idea so fast. At that time, I didn't use the "Coca Cola" script like you see everywhere now. Mine looked like this. [He wrote "*BeLLa*" on the napkin]. I sold them for €8, and they were yellow. I would have two or three hundred printed in the morning, and by 3:00 in the afternoon, they were gone. There was a time when all

4 Calling someone or something "a ball" (*che palla*) is a mildly scatological reference that implies that the person or thing is annoying, dull, or bothersome.

the American girls in Florence wanted my *Ciao Bella* tee-shirt and lined up at my *banco* to buy it. They still want those shirts! But other people watched and were jealous. Within two weeks, the Chinese started making them. They made them in every color. What could I do? I could only come up with other colors and by then it was already too late. Chinese vendors started selling them for €4 each, and I couldn't compete. Now I just keep trying to have another big idea. A shirt that says "*O Mamma Mia*," wouldn't be the same. What would you think of "Italy loves American Girls"?

Also as part of information gathering, vendors remain on the lookout for merchandise they recognize as originating from the wholesalers or artisans with whom they deal. If they spot something, they will discreetly attempt to figure out whether the competitor was given better terms. If the competitor's *banco* is close by and did not previously carry merchandise from that particular supplier, the vendor will be concerned and wonder whether the wholesaler is colluding with the rival to drive them out of business.

Wholesalers and artisans regularly visit the market to deliver merchandise, collect payment, or inquire whether a vendor would like to carry a new product. This suits most vendors, as they generally prefer not to lose time at work. As vendors also want to keep their suppliers' identities private, wholesalers often remain discreetly behind or at the side of a *banco* in order to avoid being easily spotted. Although vendors often have friendly and long-lasting relationships with wholesalers, they also note that the latter can cause them immense difficulties. Eva decries the power that suppliers hold over her, saying, "If you want to understand what it is like to be a vendor, you should follow suppliers around for a few weeks and watch what they do to us! San Lorenzo is an ocean. Vendors are the plankton; suppliers are the whales. They feed off us. If suppliers give better prices to other vendors, I won't last long here. That's why I just go directly to the wholesalers in Prato. I have to take time away from my *banco*, but at least no one knows from whom I am buying or what I paid." Eva's fears are reminiscent of Seligmann's observation in Cuzco that wholesalers may take advantage of producers through their own gathering and exchanging of information, "forming a kind of cartel among themselves to keep the prices they pay to producers low" (2004: 84).

The Best Work

I work in the market because it's the best work. I unload carts by the day, when I please, and I have no boss. And besides, the people there are the only ones I get along with and who are worth talking to (Pratolini 1968: 17).

On a day when there are lots of shoppers in the market there is little opportunity to study someone else's *banco*. On those days, Silver Street is thick with people carrying bags or dragging suitcases stuffed with purchases. One such morning, Niccolò compared the scene to a river rushing past his *banco*: "Sure, Florence has the Arno River. But San Lorenzo has a river, too. Silver Street is the river where I fish. Here I am again today, trying to catch my dinner!"

Trying to "catch" one's dinner in San Lorenzo usually involves keeping long hours. Early in my fieldwork, before I had much hands-on experience, I remarked to Ennio that he must enjoy having a job that lets him set his own hours. He looked at me incredulously and scoffed, "Choose my own hours? Any customer walking down the street sets my hours, even the ones who don't buy anything. I can't go anywhere. I can't take a vacation when other people do. Everybody else goes to the beach in August. Not me. I am standing right here when nobody else is here. In the cold, I shiver, and in the sun, I sweat. There are things I like about my work, but not the hours!"

Ennio's reaction to my naïveté underscores the fact that successful vendors make themselves as available as possible and are always on stage. As a result, some are on their feet 10 or 12 hours a day hoping to catch a customer's eye. From late autumn through the winter months, vendors are outdoors even when most shoppers consider it too uncomfortable to go to the market. Noses are red, and fingers cracked. A warm drink or a sandwich, usually taken hurriedly at a nearby bar, provides a few minutes of respite. Summer, too, exacts a toll. Florence, located in a basin between the Senese Clavey hills, is notoriously hot and humid. With warm weather come mosquitoes and "no-see-ums" that bite exposed skin. Wind poses a problem regardless of the temperature. Statues topple like dominos, papier mâché masks lose sequins and feathers, leather belts clatter to the pavement. My undergraduate research assistants who served as volunteers at *banchi* or shops also experienced long hours of hard work in difficult conditions. As one noted in her field journal, "I doubt that many people realize what a hard job the market is. You are your own boss, but you have to be working all the time trying to survive. Something as simple as eating lunch or going to the bathroom is controlled by customers. You stand, wait, and hope that you will be able to feed your family."

Discomforts and annoyances notwithstanding, many merchants are quick to point to the gratifications in their work. Ivana describes her labors as "exhausting." Still, she explains,

> It seems less exhausting when there is life in the market and the people are good. Then you notice less, even the weather. Even though it is exhausting, I love this work. I come here and see new people, new things. I can talk to other people if there aren't any customers. This is how I enjoy my life. Here there *is* life [her emphasis]. Personally, I don't shop much, just

for the things that I need. If you need shoes, a dress, you should buy them. You should buy what makes you happy, within reason. As the proverb says, "the wastrel recovers the greedy person's money." You do without all your life, then children, nieces, and nephews will waste the money of a greedy tightwad as soon as that person dies. Listen, what we do here is important work. Buying and selling makes people happy.

Ivana is not the first businessperson in Florence to espouse such sentiment. Recall that the Renaissance textile merchant Giovanni Rucellai, quoted in Chapter One, expressed nearly the same sentiment half a millennium ago. Ivana is also not the only one to be glad that her profession allows her to work independently. One slow afternoon on Silver Street, for example, I was passing time describing to a group of vendors how faculty members evaluate their colleagues for academic tenure. Dante, seizing upon an important difference he perceived between our work lives, remarked with relish, "Vendors don't have colleagues! Nobody is my colleague!" Another vendor added, "I am like a soul in limbo, but no one can tell me what to do!" Like a soul in limbo, that interlocutor did not expect his circumstances ever to improve dramatically. More important to him than a better income, however, was maintaining his autonomy. Ennio, who had responded earlier to my artless remark about setting his own hours, summed up by saying, "At any rate I am my own master. That is the most important thing."[5]

Another advantage to being a vendor, say informants, is the emotional fulfillment that comes with forging lasting relationships with neighbors and customers. Alessandra explained, "Even if this is hard work, and it is *very* [her emphasis] hard work, there is freedom. Nobody can say that I have to be here. The other important thing is the relationships. These relationships develop when you are here for a long time. They are like a kind of family relationship. If there aren't any customers, I can walk over, talk to you, then go back to my own *banco*. The people I want to talk to are all around me." Alessandra feels at ease talking with fellow vendors and customers whom she has known for years. She continued, "I say things that do not sound attractive, but nobody is shocked. If I have to, I can say, 'Wait here, I am going to the restroom.' You can say many things to people with whom you are intimate. Can you imagine a merchant in a shop saying that to a customer? But this is San Lorenzo. This is who we are."

---

5 While Dante insists that he does not have colleagues, his situation would meet the criteria of colleague proposed by Goffman: "Colleagues may be defined as persons who present the same routine to the same kind of audience, but who do not participate together, as teammates do, at the same time and place before the same particular audience. Colleagues ... share a community of fate. In having to put on the same kinds of performances, they come to know each other's difficulties and points of view; whatever their tongues, they come to speak the same social language" (1959: 160).

One expression of intimacy is the banter that many locals associate with *fiorentinità*. Florentines I know best often remark that quick, sharp wit is a key characteristic of Florentine identity. While joking and teasing entertain them, they are adamant that their humor is often strategic. Joking is their way both to demonstrate affection and to call attention to problems. One man explained, "With a joke, we Florentines move something into another kind of space and take a good look at it." A favorite tale that nicely captures this propensity began circulating after the terrible flood of 1966 that caused immense damage in the city. According to that story, elderly Lorenzo, like many others, lost nearly everything he owned. The day after the flooding finally stopped but the water in the streets was still deep, Lorenzo's neighbors glanced outdoors and saw him seated on a floating armchair that was bobbing and drifting down the street. "Lorenzo, what is going on?" they cried out." "I'm moving," the old man replied matter-of-factly. This type of joking with a point is exhibited in many contexts. An elderly woman waiting her turn with a poultry vendor remarked that she had had an upset stomach in explanation of her extended absence. The merchant feigned shock, accused her of having "betrayed him" by purchasing meat elsewhere, and then gifted her some chicken wings for a soothing broth. Pasqualino, complaining about his sore back as he wiped tables at the H13 Bar, is cautioned that the pain would be much worse if Assunta should catch him somewhere getting it massaged. George, the bread man, nicknamed for his resemblance to the American actor George Clooney, patrols Silver Street each morning fulfilling orders from his vendor clientele. Spotting him from a distance, a marketer calls out that the George he most resembles nowadays is George Washington. The bread man pauses in front of the *banco* where I am waiting for customers and remarks that he saw the first American president's dentures in a museum when he visited the United States. Rolling his eyes at me, George proclaims, "We Florentines keep the works of Leonardo in our museums! You Americans have false teeth in yours!" In typical fashion, the teasing did not stop there. A neighboring vendor who had heard us called out, "George, you've discovered America!" The vendor's interjection was intended as a jovial poke at George, because it implied that he had just said something that everyone else already considers common knowledge. These examples all carry implicit messages about issues of loyalty, disappointment, humility, culture, and identity.

The satisfaction that comes with cultivating longstanding relationships in the marketplace was also evident in Alessandra's remarks concerning what she believes her clients think of her:

> When my clients need something, they think of me. Like this boy from Prato who came and bought a pair of jeans today. He travels from Prato to Florence for a pair of jeans and comes straight to me. Of course,

there are jeans in Prato and, obviously, all over Florence. But he doesn't visit anyone else. He comes back to me. They all come back to me because they know that they can have faith in me. I know how to inspire trust; it is how I treat people, how I talk to them. They know it isn't a rip-off. If they buy, they buy! If they don't, they don't! They will come back.

Long-term vendors like Alessandra are very attentive to the interests of their regular clients. Alessandra, for example, often sets aside clothing she thinks will especially suit them, even though she could probably sell it more quickly to a stranger. Other vendors make special efforts for particular clients, too. They bring out catalogs and invite regulars to select merchandise for special order, notwithstanding that they will need to discount the shipping fee. Beatrice, for example, always makes an effort to secure new and appealing pieces for the widower who returns to her stand monthly to purchase the angel figurines that he arranges on his wife's grave. Clients obviously enjoy nurturing these relationships, too, and they sometimes stop by simply to say hello. As Counihan pointed out in her 2004 study, "For city dwellers, daily neighborhood grocery shopping was [a] way of constructing social relationships" (127), and "Daily shopping and trading ideas about cooking were important ways that Florentines connected with people beyond the family" (130). Although Counihan was referring to food shopping, the same holds true for other forms of shopping. For example, GianLuca, Alessandra's companion, remarked about the frequency of particular clients' visits with a laugh: "Sometimes they come back too much! Like that girl yesterday. She comes all the time. She parks her bike in front of our *banco* and talks to us all day! No one else can see the merchandise!" Alessandra nodded but added solemnly,

Yes, I have watched her grow up, and she always buys from me and tells me everything about her life. She started buying from me when she was 16, now she is 28. I know about her boyfriend, I know what she planted in her garden. I know what she ate yesterday and what she is cooking tonight. This is the lovely side of my work. People who can't feel what I am feeling don't understand at all. But old vendors know what I am talking about. New people just say that [working here] is too hot or too cold. There is a satisfaction that you get from being here; it is freedom, the freedom of talking to lots of people, knowing lots of people and what they want, and watching and knowing things. You can't get this feeling anywhere but San Lorenzo. My life and my relationships are close, inti-mate. We can exchange a few words. Share what we know and both be better for it. If you felt what I am feeling, you wouldn't need to ask me why I have worked here my whole life.

Lapo, who sells dried mushrooms and fruit, also tried to help me understand why relationships with clients mattered to him. He mourned how his work life has changed as relationships have become more difficult to nurture:

> Rapport and personal relationships are the most important thing in San Lorenzo. Not only because you have to make the *giornata*. Vendors extend *themselves* [his emphasis] to people through their work. *I* sell mushrooms, yes, but I am selling them to *you* [his emphasis]. You and I have now begun a relationship. Ours! Maybe we will still be talking to each other in this spot 10 years from now. But today, after the twin towers and all the bad things that are going on in Europe, people are afraid to have relationships. I greet at least a hundred people a day. I say "*Buon Giorno*," and no one responds. Maybe one out of a hundred answers me, Italians or foreigners. The tourists are scared. They hold their purses and bags close to them [he mimed clutching a bag to his chest]. What am I supposed to say to them, "Good morning, I don't want to hurt you, I'm just saying hello"? Or "Good morning, I'm not a terrorist, I sell dried mushrooms"?

Customer Relations

As a mushroom vendor, Lapo does not expect to make many large sales. Indeed, a customer who spends hundreds of euros at any single *banco* anywhere in the market would be considered a "white fly," an exceedingly rare creature. While the occasional "white fly" is coveted and becomes a story to be told and retold among friends, most transactions involve modest sums. To the longstanding vendors, this is to be expected and appreciated. Ivana states, "It all makes broth." Even €1 sales made over and over again will eventually reach the *giornata*.

To achieve the *giornata*, on good days and bad, vendors will interact with potential buyers dozens or even hundreds of times. Clifford Geertz, writing about the Moroccan bazaar where he conducted fieldwork, described the normative expectations that guide such interactions as a market's "etiquette of contact." The etiquette of contact in the bazaar was regular and predictable, Geertz explained, because market-traders "are not projected, as for example tourists are, into foreign settings where everything from the degree of price dispersion and the provenance of goods to the stature of participants and the etiquette of contact are unknown. They operate in settings where they are very much at home" (1978: 31).

For my Silver Street mentors and friends, Geertz's notion of a marketplace etiquette of contact corresponds to their idea of "the Florentine way" of conducting business. For example, interactions with customers are not

to be initiated in haste. My informants engaged customers only after someone communicated interest in a particular item, perhaps by touching it or
pointing it out to a companion, or had lingered at a *banco* for more than
one or two minutes. Then the vendor might greet the customer or make
a comment like "Lovely, don't you think?" The shopper's response, or lack
of one, will determine the next steps. If no response is forthcoming, the
merchant might try to direct attention to a slightly different version of the
same item by rearranging stock. If a shopper examined a decorated tray, the
vendor might rap sharply on a different one to show that the trays are made
of wood, or remark that these are "genuine Florentine handmade works." I
was instructed to allow customers to examine merchandise at their own pace
and undisturbed, because it is disrespectful to "throw oneself on" passersby.
Throwing oneself on a passerby can be literal as well as figurative. Niccolò,
for example, reports to owners if he notices sales assistants touching shoppers to get their attention, because it demonstrates "an ugly lack of respect
for the client and for my market."

In turn, model customers greet vendors or respond to greetings and
inquire whether they may touch an item before they actually do. Emir, who
has worked in San Lorenzo for five years, says, "If I have learned anything
from being around Florentines it is to behave when I want to buy something. I greet the salesperson. I ask if I can touch something. 'May I?' I ask,
before I pick it up. No one is saying that you have to buy anything. All you
have to do is ask and put it back where you got it." Not all interactions with
customers unfold according to the preferred norms, however. San Lorenzo
vendors more often than not attribute this unpleasantness to the fact that
short-term tourists do not understand the expectations about comportment
that are embedded in the history of this market. For example, Maso, who
sells belts and wallets, resents the fact that many tourists don't return his
greeting. "I am standing right here, and it is as if they are afraid to look at
me. They act like I am one of the poles holding up the awning." Alice, a
banco owner for 35 years, grumbled, "Customers are changing. Nowadays
people walk up, handle all my gloves. Pick them up and put them down,
pick them up and put them down. Some of them even have an ice cream
in one hand! Then they walk off and I have to clean up their fingerprints.
That never happened before." Lapo and Eva made similar points. Lapo said,
"Tourists pick up merchandise and throw it down like this [tossing a small
package of roasted peppers in oil]. When they do that, I don't even want to
talk to them. Of course some tourists are friendly and try to communicate.
I try to get along with everybody. If you don't, you won't make it here." Eva
remarked, "Here in San Lorenzo some tourists point at my scarves *with
their foot* [her emphasis; she mimicked pointing with her foot]. They have
ice cream in one hand and a water bottle in the other! 'Dear public,' I want
to say, 'All you have to do is think a little.'"

Merchants' experiences with shoppers are reflected in their character-izations of their public. The distinctions they make are imprecise but tell-ing. There are good people; people who buy/spend; polite people; arrogant people; people who break your boxes (a euphemism for the more scatological term "ball breaker," which is rarely used when discussing customers); know-it-alls; people who are never satisfied; ignorant people; tightwads; deadbeats, called the "dead of hunger"; sand heads; people who waste your time; and, nasty people, among others. Clearly these vendors have expectations about how their interactions should unfold, and some people meet them better than others.

Outdoor merchants, unlike sales assistants in department stores, are often challenged by customers to prove the workmanship and value of the merchandise they offer. Under the right circumstances, opportunities to engage in this way are welcomed by vendors as enjoyable and proud moments in their work life. Still, it can be difficult to remain polite while educating certain shoppers about quality workmanship. Akka and Niccolò, for example, often serve foreign clients who have little experience shopping for leather and do not recognize differences between the quality purses at their *banco* and cheaper ones offered by some competitors. "Feel how soft this leather is," Akka urges. "It is not hard, like dried cod. It comes from the under lay-ers of skin, not the top ones." One afternoon I eavesdropped on Akka as he attempted to correct a customer's misperception that a snakeskin purse was poorly made because the pattern varied. He pointed to different parts of the bag and said that making a large purse may require more than one snake. If the pattern across the entire purse was identical, he explained, it was prob-ably cowhide processed to look like snakeskin. The shopper looked skeptical and walked off wordlessly. Akka smacked his own forehead, then turned to Niccolò and said, "What can we say to a sand head who thinks that snakes give birth to identical twins?"

Abdul, a Bangladeshi merchant, dislikes having to convince North Americans and Australians that he is not overcharging for the silver jewelry he imports from India. "European customers understand silver," he says. "They want something that is pure silver or good quality. When a Canadian or Australian or an American comes here, they don't care about the silver. All they know is how it looks and don't care if it's silver or nickel or steel. I sell these rings at €20, but they want them for €10. I can't sell for so little, so they go someplace else where they think that they have found the same quality for €7. Every customer is not the same; some are good, and some are ignorant." Dante is driven to distraction by arrogant customers who insist that the decorations on his stock are glued on rather than painted, trying to prove it by scratching at the design with their fingernails. Ennio described a similar encounter with a "box breaker" who dismissed the provenance of his trays, accusing him of lying:

A South American turned over one of my pieces and asked, "Why doesn't it say Made in China?" "Because it is made in Florence," I told her. She said that if it were really made in Italy and not China that you would not be able to see the brush strokes. What nonsense! Are you telling me that you can't go to the Uffizi and see Botticelli's brushstrokes? Then I hear others saying that the flowers painted on Florentine trays are a copy! A copy of what? If a tray had the Mona Lisa on it, that would be a copy. Not a bunch of flowers!

Domenico, who sells Venetian glassware, reports that he, too, has occasionally run out of patience:

You can say these vases are fake, that anyone can put a "Made in Murano" sticker on the bottom of a vase. Well, that's correct. But before you tell me that the things *I* sell are fake [his emphasis], you should be able to tell me how you know. Be able to say that this color glass isn't made in Venice [he picked up a vase]. Be able to tell me that this kind of fluting isn't made only in Italy! Don't just make something up just to seem like you know something. If it costs €5, that means I paid €3 for it. Don't ask me to sell it to you for €2 … tell me where I can get a hand-decorated handmade crystal vase in Venice for €2! *I'll* buy them all [his emphasis]!

Such "know-it-alls" or "professors" pose problems because they ruin sales by offering unsolicited comments. Domenico continued,

The worst is when the professor starts talking to another customer. If they are the same nationality, the customer will believe them before they believe me, *me*, who actually *knows* this merchandise [his emphasis]. One time I lost a €55 sale: an American talking to an American. I began to put away the merchandise even before the buyer suggested it. I said "You go to Venice and see if you can find these things at this price." The customer came back the next day, but I wouldn't sell to him, I felt so insulted. "No," I said. "Go to Venice. Buy your vases there; don't buy them from me!"

Domenico's experience speaks to a point made earlier: San Lorenzo has a reputation as a budget market. One vendor laughingly pointed out the mother-of-pearl rosary he offered for €9 and commented that it was "more mother than pearl." Another showed me a poor-quality reproduction of Michelangelo's David for sale alongside better versions. He noted that the tree stump in the original reaches to just above David's knee but, in this case, the stump prodded David's posterior. Statues like that one sell well, not because the distortion from the original makes it a conversation piece, but because they are priced at €2. Interestingly, most tourists don't seem to notice the distortion.

Merchants anticipate customers' preferences as best they can, paying attention to what international tourists are wearing, how their homes are decorated in foreign television shows, what books they are reading, and what films are just arriving from abroad. In these ways, they inform themselves about new trends. When Dan Brown's 2003 novel *The Da Vinci Code* was on bestseller lists, many North Americans came searching for reproductions of "The Last Supper" that depicted Christ and Mary Magdalene seated side by side.[6] As much as vendors would have wanted to provide the picture, they insisted that it did not exist. One vendor remarked, "Hah! They can look for Mary Magdalene all they want, but they are always going to find John the Evangelist."

Vendors note furthermore that shopping behavior varies by culture. For example, Florentines are characterized as frugal shoppers who usually know exactly what they are looking for and complete transactions quickly. Visitors from the United States are the most likely to say they are "just looking" and engage in lengthy comparison shopping, sometimes circling back multiple times before finally deciding to make a purchase. Spaniards enjoy being swept up in the moment and making all their purchases at once. Turks bargain the hardest. South Asians like to discuss price but rarely complete a purchase. French customers are difficult to satisfy and speak very little. You must try to guess what they want. Americans are considered the most likely group to buy accessories customized with their own names. For this reason, a fellow who sold tee-shirts in San Lorenzo asked me to update his list of popular American women's names each year upon my return to the market. He explained, "Americans will buy anything with their name on it. I am thinking of starting a new line of tee-shirts and purses for Americans with things like 'Cindybag' or 'Cindyshirt' on them. I'm sure they will sell well!" Whether borne out in fact or simply a stereotype, these vendors work hard to be cognizant of the tendencies and peculiarities of their clients.

Tourists' clothing also provides clues to their probable shopping behavior. It was often pointed out to me that, regardless of the weather, many Americans wear "flatbreads," inexpensive plastic sandals also known as flip-flops. Canadians are rarely without at least one maple leaf patch displayed

---

6 Dan Brown's 2003 bestseller *The Da Vinci Code* and subsequent 2006 movie, directed by Ron Howard and starring Tom Hanks, both received a great deal of international attention. Although Brown's book was fiction, it included the controversial statement that Jesus Christ married Mary Magdalene and fathered a child with her, based partly on the interpretation it presented of Leonardo da Vinci's painting, "The Last Supper." That statement captured the public's imagination and also elicited strong responses from some scholars of religion and of art.

on a knapsack or toque. Turkish and Greek males wear baseball caps. Israelis usually have insulated water-bottle holders attached to their belts, and the men carry their wife's purse. Young Spaniards wear bandanas in their national colors; older ones carry backpacks across their chest. Japanese visitors are always dressed impeccably. Other tip-offs as to who one encounters are the number of children, hairstyles, and relative level of physical fitness.

Making Cents in San Lorenzo

San Lorenzo vendors face, on a continuing basis, political, economic, and social changes that can affect their livelihoods. In this regard they are no different from small-business owners throughout the world who cherish their independence and for whom providing goods and services to others results in a sense of pride and accomplishment. Some San Lorenzo vendors believe, furthermore, that they face the additional responsibility of continuing to do business in what they consider a traditional, culturally appropriate way. For them, the marketplace's erratic reputation, in particular the recent sense that it has become torn away from its cultural moorings, is upsetting. Perhaps most troubling of all is the notion that San Lorenzo has now become a sort of flea market or swap meet. The crux of their frustration is the misperception that San Lorenzo Market is more like an American-style yard sale than an assemblage of small collocated businesses operated by independent entrepreneurs who set their own prices and cultivate unique and lasting relationships with customers and neighbors. From their perspective, it is a misperception that poses a fundamental threat to their identity.

The sense that this market is seen as a kind of an international yard sale is demonstrated again and again in interactions with customers who think that posted prices are irrelevant. As part of these interactions, customers request impossibly large discounts. Compounding the financial cost of an unreasonable discount is the often impolite way in which it is requested. As one middle-aged Florentine recollected,

> Oh yes, discounts, absolutely. But we didn't say "discount" back then. We just talked about the merchandise, not the money. My mother was one who never shopped here without getting a discount. She bought my clothes. She would say to the vendor, "But what about these shorts? My son can't wear them for very long. He is growing every day. He can't wear them next year." And the vendor would say, "Signora, it is natural that a boy grows. He has to wear pants, and I have to eat." Beh! What was it to him if I grew out of the pants? But he always took a little off. It was so spirited, everyone felt satisfied, and they were glad to see my mother the next time.

Unlike in the past, however, the word discount is now heard often in the market. Beatrice said, "It amazes me. We haven't even exchanged two words and people want me to lower my price. If someone wants a better price, the way to get it is to inquire, 'Can you do a bit better?' It depends, of course, but it may be that I can lower the price a euro or two on some items." I asked an American retiree whom I served what prompted him to ask me for a 50-per-cent discount. He replied, "This place is just like the Sunrise Swap Shop where we live in Florida. In front of Sunrise there's a street with tents, just like this one. You look way up and it is all tents. The inside building is air-conditioned and the merchants pay more to be in there. They give big discounts; you just make an offer. That's how we know we'll get discounts." Some shoppers take their cue from guidebooks. A Canadian explained, "We care about price, and we want Italian merchandise. We like places we trust and know. The guidebooks say to ask for discounts from street merchants, not from shops, even though the leather shop here gave us a big discount and we didn't even ask. [She named a particular guidebook] says to ask for a discount, and so does the on-line travel guide we use. So that's what we do!" In another case a German explained, "We went to Thailand last year, and there was exactly this kind of market. You bargain a lot. They would be disappointed if you didn't try. They think it is fun!"

Remarks such as these by a well-intentioned but misinformed public point to a lack of awareness of cultural relativism expressed in the assumption that all outdoor markets are the same. Worse from the vendors' point of view is the idea that they operate as some kind of organized price-fixing cartel. A Canadian shared his perspective: "I know you have to negotiate with these fellows. But the real negotiation goes on between them. They have an understanding. Probably every morning they meet and set the prices. They work together on you. If any of them go below the cut-off price, they all have to start charging less. I would be surprised if lots of them didn't know the relationship between the euro and the foreign currencies. They're not stupid!" An American commented similarly, "Some are really aggressive, like they all have the same shtick, always haggling. And they yell at you. Well, that's ok, I respect that. I'm in marketing and I know you have to be assertive. They'll say 'I have the best leather.' I expect to haggle but it makes me uncomfortable. Usually you have to go around to a few to even begin to figure out what you should be paying. I start out with half of what they originally ask for. It's like, 'sucker!'" I asked him to elaborate. "If you don't haggle back, they think you are a sucker. If you don't beat the tar out of them, they don't respect you. It takes at least an hour of walking around this market comparing prices to catch on. I write prices down so these guys know I am not a sucker."

Thus, whereas increases in fees for use of public space or changes in rules regarding what time *banchi* must close are routine business distractions external to the relational aspects of market life, a rude demand for a discount is likely to be taken as a personal affront to a merchant's identity. The reason is that these demands occur as part of the face-to-face interactions, which, according to my sample, should be guided by norms that are direct expressions of *fiorentinità* and therefore central both to their identity and to that of the marketplace as a whole.

To recap, vendors' overall management of their time and resources is simply part of running a business. Some are better at it than others, which is why some businesses survive and others close. Increases in rent, electricity, or labor costs affect the price someone charges at a *banco* in San Lorenzo— just as they would in a shop in Florence, Italy; Florence, South Carolina; or Florenceville, New Brunswick. In that regard, these vendors see their situation as no different from that of any other small-business person, including nearby San Lorenzo merchants who operate stores. Setting a fair price is integral to their notion of how a Florentine vendor does his or her job. Therefore they are dumbfounded, for example, when tourists immediately demand a discount, which in their eyes devalues both what they have for sale and their sense of themselves as honest merchants. A purely emotional response might simply be to end the interaction, but the fact that vendors can survive only by making sales usually prevents them from refusing to negotiate. The problem with tourism, from their perspective, is not tourism *per se* but how some tourists treat them. After all, many of these vendors have already committed to selling to tourists; their willingness to do so is obvious from the wares that they offer for sale. Furthermore, as we have already seen, some vendors consider their interactions with tourists to be very satisfying. Vendors offer various explanations for why some tourists comport themselves poorly when considering a purchase, including home-country practices, guidebooks that give bad advice, prior experience at markets in developing countries, or being exposed to new San Lorenzo vendors who behave differently and then mistakenly generalizing that every vendor in the market is the same. In short, long-term vendors are not trying to treat tourists in a tourist way; they are trying to treat them in what they regard as a Florentine way, because in this market, in their eyes, that is how people build relationships of trust. How some customers now treat them in return is therefore troubling. Vendors are hoping for recognition that their price is already fair but might be tweaked, much as when a store offers the occasional single-item sale coupon. The treatment they sometimes receive, however, makes them feel diminished. In that regard, the vendors I know best were especially shocked when local clients demanded big discounts. "Give me a Florentine discount; I am no foreigner here," one woman insisted to Alessandra in reference to a pair of jeans. She countered, "No, Madam, I do not give discounts because this is not a *souk*." Reading the price sticker on a marionette, another local shopper looked aghast and demanded of Beatrice, "Don't give me the tourist price;

I am Florentine!" She replied, "Madam, I am Florentine, too. With me it is €10 for him, €10 for her, and €10 for you. What difference should it make to me where my customer is from? Doesn't anyone know how to behave here now?" Some local residents also note a change. As one woman told me, "There is a way to do things, here in Florence at least. We don't bargain much; at least we didn't when [the market] was Florentine."

This chapter has demonstrated that while *sanlorenzini* are practiced at adapting to inflows of people, growing numbers of tourists and new vendors are affecting marketplace behaviors and relations in ways that some of them associate with a decline in *fiorentinità*. Challenges to *fiorentinità* go beyond unpleasant interactions with shoppers, however. They also include tensions in vendor–vendor relations, dramatic levels of illegal vending, and, at least among licensed outdoor vendors, fresh challenges to their ability to sell merchandise in the heart of Florence, as the next chapter shows.

CHAPTER FOUR

INTO THE HEART OF FLORENCE

We must overact our part, in some measure, in order to produce any effect at all.
—Dante Alighieri

The previous chapter described many aspects of work life in the market. It pointed to the importance traditionally accorded to relations between merchants and customers, underscoring that those interactions were grounded in a normative environment that my vendor sample associates with *fiorentinità*. Thus, while the Silver Street marketers I describe seem to have a natural talent for sales, the ways in which they interact with clients are, in fact, learned behaviors that communicate and reinforce shared values. I recollect in this regard a Florentine marketer instructing his new sales assistant, "I advise you, always show respect to everyone, clients and other owners! Don't exceed the boundaries [of appropriate language/behavior]!" To do otherwise would indicate inappropriate disregard for an individual by the sales assistant and, by extension, the owner of the *banco*. By the same token, when a customer who "should know better," such as a Florentine, acts in a way that contradicts norms, people may react with surprise, frustration, or anger, as the reader will recall from the preceding discussion.

Anthropologists typically learn about norms by following the example of the subjects of their field study. Indeed, observation and experience are how people everywhere learn the norms of their group. Norms, unlike rules, are seldom written. Individuals therefore sometimes stumble and unwittingly contravene norms that, to those with more experience in a setting, are basic and obvious, as I have sometimes done. I learned firsthand that, when a slip-up concerns norms that maintain good relations among vendors, the results may be problematic. For example, one morning at the start of my third field season, I paused at a *banco* and greeted its owner casually. To my complete astonishment, the vendor responded angrily, "How dare you show me disrespect?" I asked him to explain. "Last year when you left Florence you did not say goodbye to me. I have never done anything to you and still you insulted me!" I stammered an excuse: "I asked Eva to pass along my regards." "Eva is Eva and I am me and you are disrespectful," he snapped back. I apologized and extended my hand. Two weeks later, he gave me a gift from his *banco*. We have spoken regularly ever since, and now I am much more attentive to how I behave toward vendors when I enter and exit my field site.

That example reinforces the earlier point that not meeting a vendor's expectations about appropriate behavior may be interpreted as an insult or threat, regardless of whether it was intentional. In San Lorenzo, as in other settings where people have established longstanding patterns of interaction, informal norms simply guide the way things are done. The fact that I did not know a particular norm did not excuse my behavior, because I should have known it. Indeed, though no one other than the aggrieved vendor directly chastised me for being rude, no vendor with whom I discussed that incident later ever suggested that saying goodbye had been unnecessary. One explained, "I say 'good morning' every day to everyone and get on with my own business. Doesn't cost me a cent! What people see you do in this market is as important as what they think about it." When I was working as a sales assistant at a *banco*, my presence engendered the expectation that I would behave in a normative way, even though I am a foreigner and was there only part of the time. The angry vendor probably could not have imagined that I did not know the norm and assumed, therefore, that I had intentionally ignored our relationship.

In addition to contributing to solidarity, norms serve as mechanisms of social control. During fieldwork among merchants in an Algerian bazaar, for example, Pierre Bourdieu distilled the essential qualities of a successful "market man." Foremost among them was a reputation of honor protected in various ways (Bourdieu 1977: 185–86). In San Lorenzo, too, even the hint of a snub, intended or not, is taken seriously. The market-place does not come with an instruction manual, of course, and it isn't surprising that a new entrant to this environment, including a foreigner like myself, might be unaware of some of its intricacies. Still, when its norms are contradicted, a social relationship, or the possibility of establishing one, may be foreclosed, including in cases where the transgressor was unaware that what he or she was doing was somewhere between impolite and incendiary.

Ideally, when norms governing comportment in the marketplace are observed, relationships flourish. The reader will recall that long-term vendors consider relationships to be among the most rewarding aspects of their work. As relationships take shape around buying and selling, it is instructive to keep in mind that merchants are customers, too. In the course of their workday they often purchase meals, beverages, and something to cook for dinner from a fellow vendor. My informants mentioned frequently that, whenever possible, they preferred to buy from workplace neighbors. Ivana, for instance, often reminded me that it is "better to buy from someone you know than a stranger, even if the price is the same," also bringing to mind economic historian Karl Polanyi assertion that, given the unpredictability of transactions in the marketplace, participants "aim to minimize risk ... by transforming the impersonal relationships of commercial transactions, which have neither past nor future, into lasting relationships of reciprocity" (Bourdieu 1977: 186). As habitués, vendors are confident that a barista will serve their coffee with extra flourish and no table charge, or that the greengrocer will set some of the best produce aside until vendors find a few minutes for their own shopping. Butchers and fishmongers hold back extra copies of the free morning paper delivered to their shops as a courtesy to regulars unable to claim theirs earlier. Neighboring vendors on good terms make change for one another or lend plastic shopping bags when another's supply dwindles. They keep an eye on a friend's *banco* so that he or she can run an errand. They insist that a neighbor take a pair of sunglasses at no charge on a sunny day, or gloves on a cold one. Good relations with fellow vendors are achieved and sustained when both parties follow norms of comportment that, while mostly unstated, are of enormous significance. In that regard even Dante, who had proudly announced that he does not have colleagues, encouraged me to keep in mind that, in San Lorenzo, "one hand washes the other, and both wash the face."

This chapter addresses some of the formal and informal norms that govern relations among San Lorenzo vendors. It suggests that new and greater social diversity has led to situations where local norms, in particular those that surround competition, are often inadvertently or deliberately challenged by newcomers. Transgressions frequently evoke indignation that strains interpersonal relations. Feelings of indignation have also prompted many native vendors to contemplate what it means to them to do business in a Florentine way.

The fact that more foreigners than before hold vending licenses or sublet *banchi* is not the only way in which international mobility has influenced relations in this marketplace, however. There has also been a dramatic increase in illegal vending, a practice that *sanlorenzini* strongly associate with undocumented immigration, even if not all unlicensed vendors are in fact illegal immigrants. While some forms of unlicensed vending are tolerated, extreme forms such as openly selling goods from the tops of cardboard boxes or sheets spread out on the sidewalk are not. The presence of illegal vending, many *sanlorenzini* claim, hurts licensed vendors' businesses, creates conditions for other illegal activities to flourish, and diminishes the market's *fiorentinità*.

Long-Term Vendors and Newcomers

The previous section gave an example where I transgressed a marketplace norm and had to face the consequences. Regarding the incident, recall that one of my key informants commented "What people see you do … is as important as what they think about it." His remark harks back to a distinction made in Chapter One between "front" and "backstage" behaviors in the marketplace (Goffman 1959). Another marketer offered an assessment that went directly to the heart of "backstage" behavior, pointing out that "I say hello to everyone, and then I hang this," indicating a bright red plastic chili pepper dangling discreetly from an interior beam in his *banco*. The pepper was a talisman to protect his business against *il malocchio*, or the evil eye. He continued, "Personally, I'm Florentine and we don't believe [in the evil eye]. But some people do and will try to use it to hurt [your] business. People come here from everywhere. I have to try to get along with everyone but also protect myself."[1] He added, "This market is no paradise for fools." In suggesting that he had to be particularly cautious working alongside people from "everywhere," that vendor provided insight into how he felt some aspects of social transformation in the marketplace have affected the circumstances of people like himself.

Migration to San Lorenzo from elsewhere in Italy and other parts of the world is not new. In Chapter Two I noted that San Lorenzo has historically hosted laborers and artisans from abroad. That diversity is precisely why Sabrina, the hairdresser, referred to her neighborhood as "the most cosmopolitan part of the city." Native vendors readily acknowledge legal immigrants' right to work in San Lorenzo. For example, in Chapter One I pointed out that the "San Lorenzo: A Neighborhood on the Move" exhibit that formed part of the Florentine Genius Project prominently featured images of immigrant businessmen and businesswomen, as well as Florentines. A handwritten sign that hung for a week on a wall on Saint Antonino Street made the same point more directly. Amid signs that made explicit connections between some criminal activities attributed to some immigrants, these two, addressing all non-natives, noted

"The Foreigner"   *Multi Ethnic*
The reference is directed only at   *With Legality*
Abusive delinquents
Honest foreigners
Please excuse

---

1 Migliore explains that the concept of the "evil eye" generally refers to "the ability of the human eye to cause, or at least project, harm when it is directed by certain individuals towards others and their possessions" (Migliore 1997: 13). In this instance, the charm was intended to ward off the evil eye cast by competitors who may be envious of another vendor's success. Scattering salt under a *banco* is also said to provide protection against the evil eye.

The fact that San Lorenzo Market is multicultural or multi-ethnic is often mentioned among its attractions. But whereas in the past migrants seemingly settled there for long stretches or even the rest of their lives, many now pursue only short-term economic opportunities. The results of a survey conducted in the open-air market in 1999 were suggestive in this regard. The survey characterized San Lorenzo as a tourist market and described it as a "labour space in mutation" and a "labour market for temporary integration" (Frantz 2003: 19). The dynamics of international migration could plainly be seen in the periodicity of turnovers of labor: "yesterday Rumanians, today the Mexican women, who tomorrow?" (19). Approximately two-thirds of workers who agreed to participate in the survey self-identified as "foreigners," and one-third as Italians or Florentines (4). Today, in fact, Florentines who work at this market estimate the total number of Florentine- or Italian-born vendors to be closer to 20 per cent.

Regarding encounters with diverse peoples in San Lorenzo, Ivana likes to say, "the whole world is a village"; that is, with all their strengths and weaknesses, people are basically the same all over. Still, it would appear that Ivana does not speak for all *sanlorenzini* with respect to views of marketplace comportment. In fact, *sanlorenzini* are at least as interested in the differences among people as in their similarities. Vendors speculate continually on how culture inflects marketplace performances, and long-term vendors frequently comment on their frustration with the comportment of some newcomers. Some examples follow.

The first example regards boundary maintenance. Outdoor vendors work in extremely close quarters, their carts spaced only a meter apart. I have never observed a vendor, local or otherwise, physically pursue shoppers across that space to another merchant's *banco*. Vendors where I worked even made it a point to avert their eyes from shoppers at other *banchi* to avoid any appearance of trying to entice a buyer away. One of my student assistants reported being scolded twice by the merchants for whom she volunteered for speaking to American tourists who were looking over a competitor's display. Still, respecting boundaries remains challenging because some customers, mostly tourists, walk to and fro inquiring about prices on similar items from different merchants and calling them out to family or friends. My observation has been that Florentines and other long-term vendors in these circumstances refuse to participate in merchant-baiting and simply restate the posted price when asked.

Nevertheless, wandering too far into the street to capture the attention of passersby calling out across the street or up the steps of the Central Market building were mentioned by my informants as behaviors they associate only with some new foreign vendors. Readers who have visited

FIGURE 4.1: Anonymous signage protesting illegal vending and expressing solidarity with honest foreigners.
CREDIT: Anne Schiller

markets in Italy may find it surprising that my sample described calling out to customers as problematic. Italian vendors generally have a reputation for being flamboyant. Florence itself, in fact, has noisier markets than San Lorenzo. For example, early every Tuesday a caravan of vehicles enters Cascine Park along the Arno River to set up and open the weekly market. From these rolling stores, which are actually purpose-built vans, vendors loudly hawk wares from clothing to canaries, to electric appliances, to roast-pork sandwiches. The atmosphere is markedly different from San Lorenzo. Cascine marketers extol the virtues of their merchandise at high volume to shoppers and other vendors, and they obviously enjoy listening to themselves: "Fabulous!" "Don't miss this!" "Ladies and gentlemen, here you'll find the stuff of dreams!" "Practically a gift!" Among San Lorenzo vendors, however, only elderly Italians like Silvio still occasionally call attention to their merchandise, but much more softly. Middle-aged and younger ones stand silent. I asked Beatrice why vendors in San Lorenzo don't call out in the same way. Her answer pointed to distinctions she thought were important between new and old vendors:

> All San Lorenzo vendors used to call out. Now we don't; at least Florentines here wouldn't. Things have changed. First, what we sell outside is different now. What could I say to the tourists?, "Ladies, ladies, come

look at my beautiful Davids! He comes in many different sizes!" Hah! Second, we are not all Florentines here. The way some people call out now, new vendors, is not what it used to sound like in San Lorenzo. Not at all. Some of them yell, "Lady, you, come here, and I give you a big discount. I give you 50 per cent!" If you hear that, it is just the sound of chaos. Now, if we, too, called out, we would be acting like them.

Her remark points to another area in which the practices of some new vendors conflict with longstanding norms, specifically the "discount." Many long-term vendors claim that newcomers have subverted traditional relations between buyer and seller in this regard. For example, Chapter Three quoted *sanlorenzini* who reported that "there have always been discounts" in San Lorenzo, although they did not hear the word itself used much. Dafne, who has sold Florentine paper from an outdoor cart for 40 years, shared her opinion regarding what has changed: "Clients never used to ask for discounts. If they bought a couple of items, I always rounded the number down to give them the best price to thank them. Now, most ask me for 50 per cent! People who sell small things can't give big discounts; we would go out of business." She added unhappily, "Clients have changed, but so have some of the merchants who give the impression that everyone gives 50 per cent on everything. Too bad not everyone does things the Florentine way. I am going to sell my *banco* when I just can't take it anymore."

Another vendor, Roberto, initially hesitated when I asked him to talk to me about discounts. "If you want to understand discounts in San Lorenzo, you should ask your other friends, not Florentines," he said, nodding in the direction of some new foreign vendors with whom I was also friends. I persisted, "I want to understand how Florentines give discounts." "Listen," he continued in exasperation, "discounts have been here forever. Did you see what happened at where you work just now? That polite tourist? She was supposed to pay €22. She had a €20 and a €5 note in her hand. The owner took the €20 but not the €5 and wished her a good day. That is how a Florentine gives a discount. Newcomers changed how the market operated. Now there are lots of new immigrants, and they mostly act the same. New vendors start with all their charm and trick clients into thinking they are doing them a favor with a big cut in the price. Tourists believe that's how we all behave. Florentine customers know better, even though some of them also behave badly now." Dante overheard and added, "If I wanted to, I could price everything at my *banco* at 50 per cent more, right? Logically, if I would take 50 per cent off right away, wouldn't you be suspicious about how I set my prices? Personally I wouldn't buy anything from a person who set prices that way."

FIGURE 4.2: Sign on a *banco* requesting that customers not ask for a discount.
CREDIT: Anne Schiller

Ennio told me that he felt humiliated by the turn that the market had taken: "It isn't just that they ask for a discount. It is how they do it. As if I am obligated to lower the price. If they were polite, well, I could come down a euro sometimes. When I refuse to give 50 per cent, people sometimes throw my merchandise down, shrug, and walk away. It is humiliating. I would rather starve than be treated this way." He also added that some Florentines had also begun to ask for half-price, behaving like "real louts." The impression that Florentine vendors tend to offer smaller discounts was indeed borne out in observations that I conducted together with a student assistant (Schiller and Shattuck 2011).

Long-term vendors also perceive differences between themselves and newcomers in the amount of time customers are allowed to examine goods before they are directly engaged in conversation. My key informants maintain that speaking too quickly with customers or forcing them into continued conversation while they are looking at merchandise is impolite. One of my undergraduate assistants captured this aspect of marketplace performance in his field journal: "One of the vendors that I observed today let a woman browse for what seemed like forever at her *banco* before even looking at her. Then the vendor greeted her in Italian, and the lady responded and kept looking. After another 12 minutes the woman made a decision, one apron. I thought to myself that if I were a vendor I would be angry about the customer's slowness and indecision, but the vendor did not appear to be disturbed."

Encouraging someone else's client to abandon a transaction in progress is another behavior in which long-term vendors claim not to participate and that they maintain distinguishes them from others. I was told that "walking off with someone's client is like stealing food from their table."[2] One sales assistant excitedly described the fracas that ensued when a leather vendor tried to steal another's customer:

> Did you see the police get called to my *banco* today? My boss got in a fist-fight! The fellow who rents the next stand called out to a man trying on our jackets. Told him he should look at his jackets, too. My boss stormed over. Next thing I knew they were punching one another. The one who tried to get our client to come to his *banco* tries to intimidate everyone. No respect for other vendors. Anyway, that guy is from [named a country other than Italy]. *Beh*, he is in this city now and has to make a living the way people here do.

---

2 This is not to say that long-term vendors never attempt to draw in a new vendor's customer. One morning, for example, I was preparing to buy vegetables from a business that I used to frequent on the first floor of the Central Market. The owner, originally from South Asia, turned away momentarily to take a call. Having overheard our conversation, an elderly local vendor sidled up to me and urged me to follow her, saying "We know each other," and "I have lovely squash." His call completed, the first vendor walked over to us and extended his hand for me to shake. "Come see what I have today," he cordially invited, as if we had only just encountered one another. Returning to his *banco* he waved a fragrant, freshly uprooted basil plant in front of my nose then slipped it into a bag to take home with my squash. On a subsequent visit he reminded me of the episode, noting that "it wasn't beautiful." He added, "Because she is very old and no longer herself I didn't take offense. If someone else behaved this way, I would have asked him right in front of you to tell me where my client had gone to while I was speaking on the telephone."

Finally, an area of particular contention is making disparaging comments to shoppers about competitors' wares. Ivana put it this way:

> If a customer looks at my merchandise, even if I see that they have already purchased something similar from someone else, I treat them nicely. Sometimes they show me what they bought from another vendor. I tell them it is nice, even if it is ugly. Why make them feel bad? What's done is done. And they might come back when they see how I treat people. At least they won't go back to the person saying that I criticized him. Not everyone is like me, though. Watch and see.

Ivana was correct. One afternoon, for example, I overheard a shopper bluntly accuse Dante of deception, alleging that the designs on his ceramic pieces were *appliqué* and not, as he claimed, hand painted. The shopper stated that he had gotten this inside information from another merchant. Dante became visibly upset, waving his arms and demanding furiously, "Who, who said that?" When the shopper described the source, a fellow who worked farther down the street, Dante erupted: "Listen, sir, I am Florentine. That one is not, and he is lying." He yanked his Italian identity card out of his wallet, pressed both the card and a ceramic pitcher into the surprised shopper's hands, and insisted that he examine them. With that dramatic gesture, he conveyed that the genuineness of his ceramics, his integrity, and his authentic Florentine identity were allied.

I have witnessed or heard about incidents similar to that one throughout my research. In another case a customer approached a female vendor and stated that a competitor had described her stock as poorly made. "Well, he isn't Florentine," she replied irately, "and this isn't a *souk*." In a third instance a vendor, annoyed by one of my students' repeated requests for a better price on a pair of sandals, pointed to his own face and snapped, "Miss, look at my face, my skin, my eyes, my hair, my nose. I come from Florence. On what basis do you think I am not already telling you the truth? Can you not see that I am Florentine and that you are wasting my time?"

Episodes such as these make visible the connections my key informants perceive among their business practices, identity, and *fiorentinità*, as well as what they think makes them different from newcomers. Chapter One introduced the concept of identity amplification, whereby an identity that was previously only "moderately salient" is elevated into greater significance and prominence (Snow and McAdam 2000). The changing make-up of the market, among vendors and patrons alike, has created conditions for the amplification of *fiorentinità* in some merchants' professional identity. Unlike the Moroccan *bazaari* whom Geertz (1978) described as feeling "at home" in the bazaar, few long-established San Lorenzo vendors would make the same claim today. Alessandra, who considers working in San Lorenzo the "lovely side" of her life, stated her feelings on the matter tersely: "Look, this is Florence. This is a market with a history. This is not a bazaar. I don't know why people can't see that! I think the day is coming when we will have to put up flags on our *banchi* to show that some of us are still Florentines and act like it." Resorting to such a public display might provide temporary relief for the frustrations of some, but it would surely diminish the market's overall reputation as a welcoming destination for all legal merchants looking to establish a life and livelihood in Florence.

Fixed Merchants and Infringers

In previous sections I have discussed perceptions of an increase in non-normative behavior in terms of how vendors interact with both customers and one another. My informants attribute the increase in non-normative behavior to the fact that many new vendors underwent professional socialization elsewhere and appear to have chosen not to acculturate to some practices in San Lorenzo. Thus, while international mobility has created new opportunities for some, my sample feels that their own odds of success have been negatively affected by changes in the market composition and atmosphere. As one merchant put it, "People can do what they want in their own place, [but] here we don't want to lose *fiorentinità*!"

A 2006 newspaper article entitled "Flight from San Lorenzo" was typical in how it approached the relationship between vending and *fiorentinità*. The primary interviewee, a shop owner and life-long resident, described San Lorenzo as having been formerly "the district of *fiorentinità* … with banana vendors, the old man who sold fried pasta, sausage vendors … the true ambulant vendors of Florence." Today, however, vendors

> are surrounded by kebab take-aways, call centers, gypsies on the sidewalks, extracommunitarians who sell every kind of stuff, people who relieve themselves beneath your house, unconcerned with quiet and civility, people who live for the day, devoted to doing nothing from the morning until night, whose sole intention is to encamp themselves and get drunk.

The article was accompanied by a 1970s photograph of vendors' *banchi* crowded with shoppers, when greengrocers still worked outside and the market piazza had not yet been converted into a parking lot. It was captioned, "Once upon a time: a panorama of the market about thirty years ago, a totally different atmosphere" (*Metropoli* 2006). In that article, loss of *fiorentinità* was signaled partly by "extracommunitarians selling stuff on the sidewalk" in place of "true" ambulant vendors. For the interviewee, "extracommunitarians" refers to illegal immigrants. The idea that illegal vendors lessen San Lorenzo, render it inauthentic, or pose a danger to shoppers was commonly expressed to me by informants.

Unlicensed vending is common in Florence. That fact is underscored in how vendors talk about differences among their businesses. I found it striking that they only occasionally reference the specific types of goods that they sell. Instead, the distinction they emphasize is between vendors who are "fixed" and licensed and those who are "unlicensed." The latter, known as "infringers," do not operate *banchi*. Rather, they display wares on sheets, cardboard boxes, or pinned to the inside of umbrellas. Silvio's and Dante's opinions about the difference between fixed vendors and infringers are typical. Silvio explained, "Whether a person is fixed, that's what matters. If you are fixed, you have a license, you pay rent for the space, and your *banco* is what you make of it." Dante, unable to contain his exasperation, added, "Here the most important thing is that you own a *banco*. It doesn't matter if it is the ugliest, lowest, most miserable...." He began laughing at the dismal image he had conjured of someone's imaginary business. "Anyway, the *banco* is yours, period, and you are in charge. And the infringers who come to San Lorenzo...." Silvio finished his sentence: "Infringers can go to the devil! Chaos and misery, that's what they've brought; ask anybody."

FIGURE 4.3: Irregular vendors in San Lorenzo.
CREDIT: Sarah Kim

Unlicensed Vending in the Marketplace

On any given day, dozens of irregular vendors work in San Lorenzo, and scores more are to be found in adjacent parts of the city. Some are micro-peddlers, whose merchandise all fits inside a satchel. Abdul from West Africa has frequented San Lorenzo annually for 20 years, discreetly asking vendors whether they would like to buy cigarette lighters or socks. They tease him that he must need to sell a lot of socks to support his large family; Abdul claims to have three wives and eight children. Yet enough people buy a pair to make his visit worthwhile. There are some Florentine micro-peddlers, too, including a grandmother, bent double by age, hawking packets of "Grand Finale" tissues from a battered sports bag to help support herself and her disabled son, and portly Poldo, the erstwhile doughnut man introduced in Chapter One, who resells scratch-off lottery tickets and defective stuffed toys at a small mark-up. Micro peddlers from other parts of Italy include fellows who arrive laden with bunches of dried lavender or a sack of pungent, purple garlic bulbs, freshly harvested and still covered with earth. Such periodic and episodic visits are not unwelcome.

Like micro peddlers, infringers do not pay taxes or fees for use of public space. Unlike micro peddlers, who move through the market, however, infringers attempt to occupy and hold one spot for as long as possible, often in a busy marketplace intersection, on the steps of the Central Market building, or next to a "fixed" *banco*. From that spot, they offer counterfeit designer purses, sunglasses, mobile phone covers, earbuds, and other items. Most recently, some have begun selling stolen bicycles (Conte 2014). Shoppers often must navigate around infringers to get to *banchi*, enter shops, or ascend the market building steps. The presence of illegal vendors, most of whom are said to come from East or North Africa or Eastern Europe, is a constant aggravation to my merchant sample.

As noted in Chapter One, immigration issues have taken on "great importance" throughout Italy over the last three decades (Barbagli and Sartori 2004: 172). The number of legal foreign residents in Italy has risen rapidly since the beginning of the 1990s: from 648,935 in 1991 to almost 3 million by the beginning of 2007 (Bigot and Fella 2008: 305). By 2011, the number of legal foreign residents had grown to 4.5 million.[3] At the same time, marginalized groups such as Roma (Gypsies) and asylum seekers (lately Kurds and Syrians), who do not possess required documentation, have also migrated to Italy in the hundreds of thousands. In a recent case, the Italian Coast Guard rescued nearly 1,000 undocumented migrants after smugglers had abandoned a ship

---

3 For more detail, consult the Italian National Institute of Statistics website at http://www.istat.it/en/about-istat.

transporting them from Turkey after placing the controls on autopilot (SBS 2015). As many undocumented migrants go undetected entering Italy, their exact numbers are unknown. Thus, whereas in the nineteenth and early twentieth centuries "the mobility of individuals … was viewed as a positive factor, able to generate reciprocal benefits in the economic sphere … [today] it is seen as a potentially negative factor, a harbinger of problems, insecurity and marginality" (Colombo and Sciortino 2004: 50). While many scholars have maintained that this perception is misguided, as Graziana Parati has noted, "the proliferation of complex academic investigations regarding the phenomenon of migration to Italy does not highly impact the political discourses on migration, which tend to define migration simply as a 'problem'" (2005: 148).[4]

Florence is not the only Italian city that draws undocumented immigrants seeking work. In an essay about itinerant West African vendors in Bari, Puglia, Zinn observed that these men often self-identify as "tourists" to Italy. She concluded that "[these vendors] do not take jobs from the natives; their activity is in the economic no-man's land of the submerged economy" (1994: 61). That statement is markedly different from how infringers are perceived by legal vendors in San Lorenzo, who see them as unfairly taking away income and posing a threat to public order. Vendors complain, for example, that many tourists do not recognize the difference between infringers and legal vendors such as themselves. They are correct. Over the years I have repeatedly been asked by international shoppers if the fellows with sheets are vendors who cannot yet afford to buy a *banco* and whether everyone gets their start this way. Verbal altercations and sometimes fist-fights have occurred between legal vendors and infringers during every summer I have been in San Lorenzo. From time to time, tourists who unwittingly get in the way of illegal vendors fleeing the police are hurt accidentally, or *banchi* that belong to legal vendors get damaged. As I noted in Chapter One, these episodes are sometimes described in the media as a "Far West" incident; that is, reminiscent of what life is imagined to have been like on America's untamed western frontier.

Immigrants often endure hardships during their time in Italy, and a growing body of scholarly literature addresses their experience (Albahari

---

4 Immigration to Italy rose sharply in the late 1980s, and, according to Sciortino and Colombo, by the 1990s "foreign immigration becomes the object of political controversies, legislative initiatives, academic reflections and social conflict" (2004: 102). As the press came to realize that immigration was a matter of "crucial importance for the entire social life of the country" (102), there was a remarkable increase in newspapers in the use of "immigrant" over the previously preferred and seemingly more benign term "foreigner." Many scholars have since claimed that this transition corresponds to the "increasing association of immigrants with deviance and criminality" (105). Yet Sciortino and Colombo disagree. They suggest that while immigration undoubtedly became more politicized in the late 1980s and began to be discussed in terms of social conflict, this alteration in public dialogue was instead part of a larger increase in the coverage of immigration in general and not a focus on the criminality of immigrants (110).

2010; Cole 1997; Lucht 2012). The precarious existence of illegal vendors in particular was eloquently described in an autobiography by Senegalese author Pap Khouma, *I Was An Elephant Salesman*, which became a bestseller in Italy in the 1990s (see Khouma 2010). Many people in Florence sympathize with their predicament. As one merchant commented, "Those poor souls. It is terrible for them. Some don't even come here on boats, they arrive on rafts. Some don't have many choices except to sell things illegally. They are given merchandise by a boss, and they must give back 50 per cent of what they earn. Most send nearly all the rest to their families back home. The bosses move them all around the country. But there are rules here, and if the government doesn't enforce those rules people like me cannot continue to operate our businesses in San Lorenzo." A variety of proposals have been put forward to help illegal vendors, including offering free Italian lessons and temporary work permits. Several years ago the Florence City Council attempted to ameliorate relations in the marketplace by employing "cultural mediators" to broker communications between illegal and regular vendors. Some residents take a much dimmer view of the presence of illegal workers, however, and are not in favor of extending special considerations and assistance.

In 2010, after a brawl broke out between registered market vendors and unlicensed vendors from Senegal, the city's leadership organized an open meeting between licensed vendors and representatives of the Senegalese

FIGURE 4.4: Irregular vendor next to a sign forbidding the purchase of counterfeit goods.
CREDIT: Anne Schiller

community. The licensed vendors wanted financial restitution, €1,800, for a vendor whose *banco* had been particularly damaged. One counterproposal offered by a spokesperson for the undocumented vendors was that their community host a communal West African–style dinner in the marketplace piazza to promote harmonious co-existence. A member of the Senegalese community commented, "Yes, there are other things that these young men could do, paint houses or work in construction, but who will give them a chance? And many of them read books and study hard while they are here, and send money home. They need help." Akka, the purse vendor, asked to speak. "I am from Iran," he said. "I have been here for 27 years. The things that illegal immigrants do today, I myself have never done. I respect Italian laws. Now I am frightened for my customers. Fist-fights and running through the market is not what San Lorenzo was like before. What if one of them runs into a pregnant woman?" The meeting did not succeed in reducing tensions, nor was the issue of restitution or even dinner settled at that time. Participants on both sides left feeling frustrated. I headed back to the market with a group of long-term merchants. One called out to an illegal vendor, "You want my job? I'll sell you my *banco* right now." The latter responded sharply, "I don't want your *banco,* and I don't want to stay here the rest of my life. I would rather sell drugs than work here forever like you." "You heard that, right?" the vendor asked me. "Would you put that in your book?" Their angry exchange highlights some of the current strains and complexities in the market. On the one hand, long-term legal vendors have made business decisions and financial investments that provide them the opportunity to compete for customers, including tourists, in this busy marketplace. On the other hand, illegal vendors flock to San Lorenzo precisely because it provides a continuous flow of potential clients. It simply would not make sense, given their situation, for them to bother to display their merchandise on a street devoid of tourists, or in a park in some corner of the city. This example points to a fundamental difference in perspective. What a *banco* owner fears to be a continuing set of conditions with little hope of relief, an illegal vendor may see as a short-term situational opportunity and necessity.

In 2009, the City Council began issuing aluminum markers to identify *banchi* operated by registered vendors. In addition, several large signs in multiple languages were mounted in the market zone notifying shoppers that they would be fined if they were apprehended making a purchase from an illegal vendor. Some infringers were undeterred and set up cardboard boxes or spread out sheets alongside the signs to take advantage of the shade created by their height. Eva, who arrived at work to find one of the signs close to her *banco*, remained skeptical: "That big sign [next to my *banco*] won't change anything. This used to be an Italian market, you know. Now it practically belongs to illegal sidewalk vendors who make life miserable for every immigrant. Legal immigrants like me have to eat, too."

Sanlorenzini do not attribute a perceived rise in incivility and petty crime solely to the illegal vendors, although many suggest that such concerns are linked to a growing problem of illegal immigration generally. Chapter One, for example, contained the tale of the cinema manager who claimed fear of immigrant crime as the reason why city residents avoided going to the movies at night, leading to the failure of his business. The demand that city officials take action to end illegal activity is certainly a popular subject for signage, as demonstrated in this anonymous poster, written in imperfect English, mounted on an electrical pole on Silver Street:

CHAOS AND PURSE-SNATCHING

STABBINGS

FILTH-DEGRADE

INCIVILITY

AUBUSIVENESS

ILLEGALITY

ABBANDOMENT

DELINQUINCY

ENOUGH

Another sign that hung for a week on nearby Faenza Street read:

Businessmen, Residents and Merchants in San Lorenzo
    Ask the City Government of Florence to restore the quality of life and basic rights of citizens by solving, as quickly as possible, the following problems:

1. Unauthorized gambling (the shell game)
2. Drugs and Drug Selling
3. Unlicensed vending ...

We require strong action from the authorities to re-establish legality

Building upon earlier work by Stanley Cohen, Goode and Ben-Yehuda (1994: 31) have theorized the notion of "moral panic," defined as "the feeling, held by a substantial number of the members of a given society, that evildoers pose a threat to the society and to the moral order as a consequence of their behavior and, therefore, 'something should be done' about them and their behavior." While there is evidence of significant criminal activity attributable to irregular immigrants throughout Italy (Faesani 2009), the heightened concern in San Lorenzo is linked to some local events. One was the attack on Lina, former caretaker of Saint Joseph's Oratory on Saint Antonino Street, cited at the opening of this book. More recently, an Iranian shopkeeper filed a police report after she was shoved and threatened by an illegal vendor who became angry when she asked him to leave the steps of her shop. The next morning, a delegation of other irregular vendors from the same country as the man who had threatened the shopkeeper visited the woman and explained that the man who had frightened her was an outsider to their group. The newspaper described the uneasy state of affairs as "symptomatic of relationships that have become stormy ... of a longstanding tolerance put to the hard test" in what is becoming an "off-limit zone" with a growing sense of "moral and social degradation" and insecurity (Gianni 2013: 3).

To attract greater attention to their problems, some *sanlorenzini* document the episodes of illegality and incivility they see and disseminate them on social media. Examples include videos entitled "Gypsies [Play] Scratch and Win in the Market Piazza" and "Piss in San Lorenzo." These and others have found their way through social media into the public sphere.

Talking to the Neighbors

> This market is the very heart of this city. But look what happened here. The city's heart is broken!
>
> —a San Lorenzo shop owner

This chapter has suggested that there is a rise in non-normative interactions in San Lorenzo as well as illegal vending that, rightly or wrongly, are associated with the perception of an increase in other crimes. As a result, many different types of social relations across cultural boundaries are at risk. Among the anthropologists who have theorized the role of non-normative interactions and social breeches in initiating social change is Victor Turner, who pointed out that disputes have a "life cycle" that run their course through situations that are both chronological and typological (1960: 239). He posited that non-normative interactions are important in part because they encourage reflection on the conditions that led to a breech in relations, and that awareness of what caused a breech is necessary to redress it.

This kind of reflection is underway in San Lorenzo. But what mechanisms could be put in place to reduce tension or redress ambiguity over normative behavior remain unclear. Mansour, a San Lorenzo vendor who arrived 20 years ago from Iran, commented on this uncertainty:

> The market has declined partly because there are lots of different cultures here and they don't mix all that well. There are so many quarrels. Vendors look friendly, say *ciao*, slap one another on the back, but then one of them does something that another cannot accept, and then they can't

stand one another. Some [foreign vendors] are at fault. Our undoing is some employees who ignore how people here do things. Then there are the illegals. Nobody should have for free what the rest of us work like dogs to get. But Florentines are at fault, too, when they exaggerate [about immigrants and crime]. You know, I've been to Mexico on vacation, and if all the stories told about tourists having their cameras stolen by Mexicans are true, then everyone who has ever gone there is missing a camera! Same thing here. But the fact is, we talk to the people we know. In San Lorenzo, people don't really know one another. At least not now.

On various occasions I have asked Florentine vendors if they have ever spoken directly with new vendors about their marketplace techniques and the possibility of finding common ground. Roberto the tee-shirt vendor's answer was typical: "No. I have not because, at the end of the day, everyone goes home and eats in his own house." In other words, he did not anticipate developing sustained relationships with these new arrivals. For now, the relative lack of effective channels of communication among vendors and residents with different origins keeps the odds of deeper sociocultural integration low.

Yet in spite of the challenges, there is evidence to suggest that greater integration could be realized. I recall in this regard a conversation with GianLuca and Alessandra about diversity on Millet Street. GianLuca told me,

> A reporter came here after one of the big fights with the infringers and wanted to ask me questions about integration and racism. I told him that I did not want to talk about racism; I wanted to talk about legality. The reporter kept asking, "Is there racism in San Lorenzo?" I said, "What racism?" Look around, Chinese own the *banco* next to ours. They have a license and they are legal. They follow rules and never do anything stupid. They have their clients, I have mine, and we don't make things hard for one another. They say they want us to visit them in China. We babysit their son; his Italian name is Sandro. Before they came, their uncle and aunt worked here for six or seven years. Across the street is a Bangladeshi. Over there a Pakistani. We all cooperate. See that Iranian fellow whose leather shop is on the corner, the fellow who just waved? Last Friday, during that terrible rainstorm, his shop flooded. I closed my *banco* early, at 4:00 p.m., and helped him clean up. If an infringer makes trouble in San Lorenzo, people say that we are racist. But what if I don't make sales and decide that I might do better in Piazza Repubblica? Can I just roll this *banco* across town and start selling clothing in front of the Hard Rock Cafe? I would be arrested. If I can't make money here, I can't go anywhere else. We are not racist, but we have rules. When people follow them, everyone has a chance to succeed.

As the chapters of this book have shown, *sanlorenzini* largely agree about the types of problems that affect this neighborhood. The majority are adamant that San Lorenzo Market is in difficulty and requires improvements. But what "Saving San Lorenzo" actually means, how it should be done, and who can do it, continues to be debated, as the next chapter reveals.

CHAPTER FIVE

SAVING SAN LORENZO

> If we want things to stay as they are, things will have to change.
> —Giuseppe Tomasi di Lampedusa

The San Lorenzo Market is iconic for many reasons. The market building, a nineteenth-century architectural marvel, evolved over time into a lively twentieth-century commercial center for the working and middle classes and eventually one of Florence's top 30 tourist destinations. Its tradition of outdoor vending stretches back even further. *Banchi* have furnished housewares for countless homes, provided clothing for generations of families, and also become a destination for innumerable tourists. As the number of shoppers increased, so too did the number of *banchi*. For many Florentines, San Lorenzo still conjures images of a place where the nostalgic ideals of *fiorentinità* were realized in the most basic activities of daily urban life: buying, selling, and chatting with neighbors. Its actual history is, of course, less idyllic; recall that the market building was constructed partly to enable authorities to monitor some of the inhabitants of a worrisome part of town. To be sure, no one I know has claimed that life in San Lorenzo was ever perfect. Still, people tell me that there was something quintessentially Florentine about San Lorenzo Market, something that, unlike warm unsalted bread, freshly slaughtered chickens, supple leather gloves, and lustrous woolen scarves, is simply no longer there.

Regardless of whether notions of San Lorenzo's former *fiorentinità* are predominantly influenced by genial retrospections of the middle-aged and older, few people are content with its current state. The owner of a housewares store put it plainly: "Florentines don't come here anymore. One by one people are giving up. Soon there won't be any Florentines left. The things that we face in this market, we cannot put up with! My husband and I are also thinking of moving." That shop owner no longer felt she belonged in San Lorenzo.

The idea of belonging is important to anthropologists who want to understand how people "mobilize and crystallize [identity] at particular moments in history" (Lovell 1998: 6) and how "uses of the past can indicate ideal future choices" (Parkin 1998: xi). As previous chapters have shown, in San Lorenzo, history, shared sentiments, and habits associated with *fiorentinità* have contributed to a sense among my informants that they belong there. Belonging in the context of being a long-term vendor is at least equal to having been born in this neighborhood. In that regard, responses I received when I asked some of my informants gathered in the H13 Coffee Bar why they thought long-term residents and vendors considered leaving were illuminative. Jacopo spoke first: "You don't hear people speaking Florentine here anymore, like they did when I worked for my grandfather." "So is *fiorentinità* just a different way of referring to Florentine dialect?" I prodded. "You are saying that people would just rather be somewhere with others speaking *fiorentino*?" "No, it's not just the words," declared Silvio. "It is the way we use them. Remember, this is a market. It isn't a place of noblemen and rich people. Sometimes we curse, make jokes, we swear. But in San Lorenzo we understand each other." I asked, "So *sanlorenzini* express a sense of community by how they talk to one another?" Ennio joined in. "We did before. You used to hear our way of speaking and knew that you were in San Lorenzo. You called out to people and they answered you. Sometimes you heard a little English, but mostly you heard Florentine. Now you hear foreign languages, but nobody talks." Alessandra explained, "So, you see, it isn't just the language, really. How we talked went with what we did. We spoke Florentine, kids played in the streets, people ate ice cream, and we laughed together. When we weren't working we still came out because here is where we wanted to be. Now San Lorenzo is quiet. Nobody is here." By nobody Alessandra meant, of course, people among whom she felt she belonged. As the members of the little group headed back to work, Silvio, who was actually born across town, threw in, "People like me belong to this market, and the market belongs to us."

Silvio's aside warrants deeper consideration, because it helps us to better understand the multifaceted perceptions of who "belongs" in the market and why. Thus far in this book we have followed an unfolding story of stability and change. Predictably, the San Lorenzo neighborhood and the marketplace at its heart historically reflected the habits of the majority of its inhabitants—that is, a subsection of Florentines. Yet change has come in the form of newcomers to the city in general, and to the San Lorenzo neighborhood in particular, over the course of hundreds of years. Diversity, then, is also basic to the make-up of this neighborhood and market. Seen in that light, Silvio's comment regarding "people like me" and "belong(ing) to us" is all the more nuanced. By "me," Silvio certainly refers to his family's own Florentine ancestry and vendor lineage. But we know, as Silvio and the other long-term vendors who work alongside him know, that in another sense the "me" to whom he refers in multicultural San Lorenzo is not necessarily restricted by birthright or nationality. That "me" refers to those who have embraced the traditions and values of this Florentine marketplace and put them into daily practice by their comportment. Those traditions and values, in the eyes of Silvio and many others, were reflected in the norms of this marketplace in its prime, when people looked forward to the annual watermelon feast or to coming back to chat when they were not working, when it felt familiar and familial, when the people around them behaved like they expected. The notion of "us" is equally subtle. "Us" includes vendors of many shapes and sizes; it can mean anyone who makes their living (legally) at a *banco* and adheres to the norms. Silvio's *fiorentinità* can exist in even a diverse and changing market environment, if people permit it.

In Chapter Four I suggested that the key concerns of long-term San Lorenzo vendors like Silvio today are lack of shared norms, illegal vending, and the perception of a rise in crime that deters some people from wanting to go there or to remain. Long-time neighborhood residents would agree with vendors on all of these points. For example, various San Lorenzo neighbors over many years have told me that they have felt appalled by some behaviors they have witnessed or heard about, and they are concerned about risks they would not have considered possible a generation ago. Like my vendor sample, they also express nostalgia for a time when the marketplace, at least in their minds, was a better fit for the neighborhood's Florentine ambience. As Bromley has aptly noted regarding the urban Global South and beyond, however, "[t]he street is both a contested space and a space for contested visions where different uses and activities, both real and envisioned, compete for significance" (2013: 25). Unlike vendors, many residents also criticize the marketplace landscape, stating that the large number of outdoor enterprises makes them feel penned in, assaulted by noise, and overwhelmed by crowds of tourists. For those reasons, they question the extent to which the presence of so many outdoor vendors is essential to maintaining or restoring *fiorentinità*.

Thus it remains to be resolved whether the San Lorenzo Market is sustainable, and if it is, in what form. When I launched this project a decade ago, "Save San Lorenzo" was a rallying cry. While fewer people now use those words specifically, activities germane to the slogan continue. In fact, they have coalesced into a diffuse social movement that has generated many citizen committees and business consortia where memberships sometimes overlap. As Diani has pointed out for other contexts, it is useful to trace those connections as well as to note their absence in order to understand the dynamics of a movement in progress (2004: 352).

Due to the committed efforts of individuals, citizen and merchant committees, and civic officials who have tried to address some of their various concerns,

San Lorenzo is unquestionably better maintained and better serviced than when I first visited. Still, rival visions for its future set some vendors, residents, and other business owners at odds. For example, the goals of those who would like to see San Lorenzo regain its local popularity as a good place to shop and live are practical as well as notional. The former include promoting business, increasing access to services, enhancing public safety, providing better sanitation, and showcasing more public events such as films, exhibits, and concerts. Notional goals include promoting intercultural harmony in what clearly is now a very multicultural environment, and, among some stakeholders, restoring *fiorentinità*. Yet while the term *fiorentinità* is used by many, it is deployed differently by a range of stakeholders who hope for different end results.

For instance, unlike my vendor sample, some residents argue that it is precisely the presence of a large, crowded outdoor market such as San Lorenzo has become that sets conditions for social problems to germinate. Just as the possibility of informal-sector labor attracts illegal workers, they reason, large-scale ambulant vending lends itself to creating circumstances that diminish *fiorentinità*. Those who hold that opinion do not put too fine a point on a merchant's origins, Florentine or otherwise, emphasizing that, until recently, San Lorenzo was simply a place with fewer vendors and, consequently, fewer day laborers. According to this bloc, which includes some residents and shop owners, reducing the number of outdoor vendors and managing their activities more closely would create a less crowded market, draw more local residents, and reduce San Lorenzo's attractiveness to a criminal element. One resident explained, "The market is changing and I believe it is partly vendors' fault. They cater to tourists, not people like me, real Florentines." Another observed,

> Vendors can tell you anything, sure, although new ones exaggerate the worst. Once on my way to the Central Market I heard a vendor tell a boy that a coat was special because it was made from "genuine Canadian bison worked by real Florentine artisans." Real Florentine artisans who were born in China and live 10 to a room in Prato, I bet! Well, maybe that's terrible [for me to say], but, look, it isn't all the immigrants' fault. So many Florentine vendors have already sold their business licenses to foreigners. They don't have to; they just do. They want cash. They could pass their *banchi* to their children. If local vendors want local customers, they have to do more to keep clients like me. They should do business here like it used to be done, with *fiorentinità*!

Some residents list among the downsides of ambulant vending the fact that *banchi* are noisy (their wheels clatter on the stone streets) and sometimes unattractive (by their standards), and that they impede shoppers' views of other merchants' storefronts, thus "burying them alive."

One retailer, described by a local paper as "having a business practically walled in," commented, "We are hidden ... and when it rains the awnings of the vendors' stands fill up with water, and it pours out on the shops. In the past, it wasn't that way. Even though the market was always there ... it was different because between one *banco* and another there was space to pass through. Now, instead, it is as if we work in a cave" (Ressa 2011). Retailers with similar views have sometimes hung banners high on the exterior walls of buildings where their enterprises are located that read "SHOPS ARE WALLED IN ALIVE" and "MORE VISIBILITY [IN ORDER] NOT TO DIE."

For years some activists have promoted the view that the market needs physical reconfiguration and repurposing of space. It is in gradually moving toward the realization of that objective that a paradox has become increasingly apparent. Specifically, some *sanlorenzini*, including most long-term vendors, feel that legal ambulant vending is a foundational part of San Lorenzo's *fiorentinità*. Others maintain that restoring *fiorentinità* or at least a greater degree of decorum to the market zone calls for a drastic reduction in the number of outdoor enterprises and perhaps the relocation of those vendors who opt to remain to fixed ornamental kiosks, called architectonic *banchi*. This type of *banco* is already in use in some other nearby venues, for example, at the entrance to the Piazza dei Miracoli in Pisa, where the Leaning Tower is located.

A Neighborhood Association

The polemics that surround improving livability in San Lorenzo reveal differences in how stakeholders think *fiorentinità* is best preserved or demonstrated. Over the years, various organizations and committees have contributed perspectives and ideas to this very public debate. Among them is a prominent non-profit neighborhood association called "Together for San Lorenzo," which was established in 2004. Its membership is composed mostly of neighborhood residents, and its charter is based on the principles that *sanlorenzini* have the "right and duty to signal ... danger and degradation, not to passively accept ... abuses and injustices, and, as far as possible, to utilize the means at [their] disposal to resolve the thousands of problems and daily obstacles to the livability [of this] neighborhood." Its goals include the "environmental, cultural, economic and social requalification" of San Lorenzo, and "cultural support for the realization of social, cultural, and environmental events and initiatives and neighborhood improvement."[1]

---

1 For more information on "Together for San Lorenzo," see the organization's home page: www.insiemepersanlorenzo.it/, or Facebook page; https://www.facebook.com/Associazone-Insieme-per-San-Lorenzo-246708508769242/timeline

Since its inception it has proposed or lent support to several projects aimed at the requalification, or regeneration, of neighborhood assets, among them the repurposing of the first floor of the Central Market building and the redevelopment of the former Rex/Apollo Theater on National Street as a luxury hotel.

Together for San Lorenzo has reaped impressive results from its efforts. Partly in response to one of its early campaigns, for example, the City Council approved limits on the hours of evening alcohol sales by local mini-markets. In addition, after heavy lobbying on the part of the association, the city funded major infrastructural improvements including repaving several battered streets. I became acquainted with "Together for San Lorenzo" when I attended a special meeting called in the wake of a particularly fierce 2007 skirmish between legal vendors and infringers. The agenda at the first meeting I attended included brainstorming strategies to cope positively with social change. The focus of the discussion was on creating a more explicitly multicultural identity for the neighborhood. One suggestion for a step in that direction appeared on a handout circulated at the meeting. It was to launch a series of public meetings in the piazza, weekly or every ten days, on topics including racism, antiracism, and civic coexistence. Such occasions would involve the advice of foreigners in the town and province.

Since its inception, Together for San Lorenzo has hosted or collaborated with local businesses on a range of neighborhood events, usually with social, cultural, or environmental themes. An example was a very well-attended 2009 community clean-up day that was also intended to promote greater social integration among locals and newcomers. Called "Let's Make Ourselves Beautiful," it portrayed San Lorenzo as a neighborhood that embraces diversity. The event was staged mostly in Pinocchio Park, a small park next to the market piazza that honors the legacy of the author and former San Lorenzo resident Carlo Lorenzini, who, under the pen name Carlo Collodi, wrote *The Adventures of Pinocchio* (1883).

To prepare for "Let's Make Ourselves Beautiful," at least a dozen banners with multicultural messages were unfurled from the upper stories of apartment buildings adjacent to the market piazza. Among them were images of a rainbow over an imaginary San Lorenzo skyline; different-colored figures rebuilding the church; different-colored hands interlaced around the church; four differently dressed human figures, including two women in traditional African dress; and a row of houses, each in different colors. Among the entertainments was a tea ceremony enacted by a performance artist who demonstrated the art of preparing and serving tea according to multiple cultural traditions. The afternoon culminated with a symbolic sweeping of the piazza by neighborhood children, followed by a communal meal. Speeches by organizers emphasized the need for the city to dedicate resources toward improving the zone. The signage that formed a backdrop to the podium addressed the same theme. One read "The Market Piazza is in a state of indignity for those who live there, work there, and for foreign guests in Florence." Another conveyed, "San Lorenzo is 'Special' with the greatest number of Shops, Tourists, Foreigners, and Hotels … Spectacular Action is Needed."

FIGURE 5.1: United Colours of San Lorenzo banner at the "Let's Make Ourselves Beautiful" event sponsored by Together for San Lorenzo.
CREDIT: Anne Schiller

The Saint Orsola Project and the Search for "Monna Lisa"

To promote social integration and improve quality of life on the scale it envisions, Together for San Lorenzo seeks an appropriate events space. For that purpose, it has long championed the renovation of the former Convent of Saint Orsola, another of the association's key neighborhood requalification projects. Located a scant three-minute walk from the Central Market building, Saint Orsola is an enormous complex, quite decrepit, about the size of a city block. Originally founded in 1309 for the Benedictine Order, it was later transferred to the Franciscans. Over the 700 years since its construction, in addition to being a sanctuary, the space has been used as a tobacco-processing facility, a homeless shelter, extra classroom space for the University of Florence, and a Customs and Tax Office. At one point it barely escaped being razed to make way for a new parking garage. Today, however, most of Saint Orsola's massive arcade is bricked shut. With its exterior crumbling and sometimes marked with graffiti, the edifice is in dire need of restoration. Together for San Lorenzo is among the organizations that have spearheaded the campaign for Saint Orsola's restoration as a multicultural community center that hosts artistic performances, sports activities, and reading and discussion groups. By 2007 the proposed repurposing had already won the support of then-president of the province, Matteo Renzi, who described his interest in seeing the former convent turned into "a high quality education center. We hope to move the arts high school there, making Saint Orsola and San Lorenzo the natural end of a triangle of beauty that touches the Medici Palace, the Accademia and San Marco on one side, the Uffizi Gallery and the Town Hall on the other. Saint Orsola will host studio space for grand artists and places for cultural production" (Vanni 2007). The significance of Saint Orsola was also underscored in the 2008 "San Lorenzo: A Neighborhood on the Move" exhibition and described as a "lost piece of the urban fabric" (Filardo and Savorelli 2008: 1). Among the aspects of Saint Orsola that add interest and upon which the neighborhood might capitalize, is the issue of who may be interred beneath the building. Ongoing archaeological excavations inside the structure may eventually prove successful in locating the remains of former neighborhood resident and convent benefactress Lisa Gherardini. Gherardini is widely believed to have been the subject of Leonardo da Vinci's early-sixteenth-century masterpiece *La Gioconda*, or *Mona Lisa*, which is now housed in the Louvre Museum in Paris.[2] The remains that have been

---

2 In 1503, Gherardini and her husband, silk merchant Francesco di Bartolomeo di Zanobi del Giocondo, purchased a house on Stove Street (*via della Stufa*), which today faces the back of the Central Market building. *La Gioconda*, the title of da Vinci's famous painting, is a feminized version of Lisa Gherardini's husband's family name. The term "Monna," a polite title for noblewomen in the Renaissance, is generally preferred in Italian to "Mona."

previously exhumed from the site and tested have not yet been conclusively identified as those of Gherardini (Tabegna 2015).

Excellent intentions aside, the former convent's renovation has not made as much progress as hoped over the past decade, an issue linked partly to cost. The City Council has approved the renovation plan in principle but has not earmarked funding for it. Attempts to find private funding continue.[3] As a spokesperson for Together for San Lorenzo remarked at a 2013 press conference, "As we have always said, once we resolve [the situation regarding] Saint Orsola, we will have resolved many things," adding, "Saint Orsola is not an abandoned dream." More recently, in 2015, Together for San Lorenzo sponsored a photographic exhibition entitled "San Lorenzo. The Magnificent Stones, the Heavens, the Forsaken. A Photographic Tour of a Changing Neighborhood," which highlighted images of some important neighborhood buildings including Saint Orsola. According to the exhibition flier, "[Saint Orsola's] reclamation, currently in progress, will be among the most important moments in the urban redevelopment of the San Lorenzo neighborhood." Among the other organizations involved in promoting the renovation of the former convent is the Academy of the Fine Arts of Florence (l'Accademia di Belle Arte di Firenze), which hosted the exhibition "Ecco Sant'Orsola" there, also in 2015 (Gori 2015).

Together for San Lorenzo has other dreams it hopes to realize in this neighborhood as well. As an officer remarked, "'Beauty, Legality, and Viability' has practically become our motto." An aspect of the organization's overall plan for the zone that is extremely provocative in the eyes of ambulant vendors, however, is the support that it and some others in Florence gave to efforts to remove *banchi* from the immediate environs of the San Lorenzo Church, as well as other changes in the configuration of outdoor vending. A document prepared for civic officials to consider noted that "abandonment on the part of residents, the progressive 'desertification' [of the zone], the worrisome fluctuations of use for the Central Market, [and] the declining quality of the goods for sale in the direction of globalization, shout out for a reversal of current tendencies" (Associazione Insieme Per San Lorenzo n.d.). It offered several suggestions to counteract the current trend. Recommendations included using the piazza behind the market building for cultural activities, including outdoor films; removing all *banchi* from the San Lorenzo Church piazza; and restoring the first floor of the indoor market to permanent uses that benefited residents, tourists, and merchants, rather than

3 For more on the association's efforts toward the renovation of the former convent, see *La Nazione* (2010), and Vanni (2013: VI). For more on the city's decision to renovate the building, see: http://dominoweb.comune.fi.it/OdeProduzione/FIODEWeb1.nsf/AttiWEB/5357 F784339DC71FC125786F002A5AA8/$File/2011_C_00015.pdf. For more on initiatives to support the restoration of the building, see santorsolaproject.blogspot.com.

FIGURE 5.2: Exterior view of the former convent of Saint Orsola during Vaclav Pisvejc's 2012 art installation. The decorative materials used were reproductions of American dollar bills.
CREDIT: Alamy

leaving it closed except for special events. Other proposals included reducing the length of the ambulant vendors' *banchi* by about 20 inches to reduce congestion and create more space between them, varying the geometry of *banco* placement so that shops are more visible, or, as stated in the document, "let[ting] the shops breath[e]," putting esthetic standards in place to improve the look of *banchi*, and requiring rubber tires and motors for each *banco*.

For their part, many in my vendor sample interpreted some of these proposals as putting their livelihoods at risk. They argued that some proposals failed to take into sufficient account the importance of ambulant traditions, which are, in their eyes, an integral part of San Lorenzo's *fiorentinità*. They demanded more adequate consideration of the situation that vendors face and of their important economic contributions to this neighborhood and city.

Tsunami on the Market Stands

In previous chapters I noted that operating a *banco* is an expensive proposition, considering the cost of a vending license or sublet, the price of a *banco* and the expense of garaging it, investment in merchandise and its storage in a warehouse, and other factors. In Chapter Three I remarked that fees for the use of public space nearly doubled a few years ago. Not surprisingly in the face of that staggering increase, vendors registered swift opposition, picketing City Council meetings and holding a one-day general strike

(*Corriere Fiorentino* 2010). Some predicted glumly that increased fees were a portent of things to come, and that the city was actually intent on driving them from the marketplace entirely. Beatrice explained at the time, "If this is what is happening, and maybe it is, I don't know anymore, it is idiotic. The city thinks it can do what it likes, but it is idiotic to chase ambulants out of this market. It doesn't consider San Lorenzo a historic market, even though vendors like me have been on these very streets for hundreds of years. Every city in the world has a market. This one is the market of the Florentines, so why is the city trying to drive the last Florentines away?"

Jacopo was convinced that the city was not only trying to remove the outside vendors. He contended that after the marketplace's first-floor renovation was complete, he and others like him would not be invited to return. "The city wants high-end shops, Gucci and Cavalli," he said. "It wants fashion shows on the first floor, not people like me. What happens to somebody like me? People like me lose our businesses and just end up washing dishes somewhere." Some vendors took to blogging and social media to express their frustration. One vendor, addressing his remarks to civic officials, posted on social media:

> I work in San Lorenzo … I am a pushcart vendor … I sell florentine handiwork that is of better quality than what they sell in historic center shops. I am a florentine and lived in the historic center when those who lived there were the true florentines, straightforward and simple. I, dear gentlemen, work every day with my wife at my *banco*, working my ass off from eight to seven, eating a sandwich at my *banco*. I pay the highest tax for use of public space anywhere in the world … all of the taxes that are imposed to operate this kind of activity, in the sun, the wind, the rain, the cold, the heat … all of this sometimes for just a few euro a day…. I am astonished [by how the city treats licensed vendors].

Anger at the fee increase paled in comparison, however, to the uproar generated in 2011 when city officials signaled their intent to drastically reduce the number of *banchi* in San Lorenzo by about 80 by not renewing some vendors' licenses.

An ambulant vendor's license to operate in Florence is subject to renewal every ten years. Of the nearly 250 outdoor vendors who formerly held licenses in San Lorenzo, 90 per cent were scheduled to apply for license renewal at the end of 2011. The original plan to reduce the number of *banchi*, vendors advised me, did not include the option to transfer operations to other parts of Florence. Indeed, strategic cuts were planned throughout the city. In total, 247 ambulant licenses would not be renewed, reducing the number of *banchi* in all of Florence by almost half (Marchini 2011). Unlike San Lorenzo, the New Market, ten minutes away by foot, would be unaffected. Some civic leaders suggested that these closings would effectively "liberate" several of the most important public squares, San Lorenzo included. But vendors were infuriated. The following open letter to the mayor, written by "Stefano" and entitled "Listen to Us Ambulant Vendors," was typical:

> I don't know how to describe to you my desperation from when it came out that you wanted to take our work. Probably you won't see it from this point of view but, by all effects, that's what it is. I would like [to ask] that you truly meet those who work every day in San Lorenzo ... I can assure [you] that they merit greater consideration. People who work their whole lives every day for 10–12 hours a day, forced to struggle with illegal vending and economic crisis that have further reduced receipts in recent years. There are things that need to be changed, that's true, and lots of them ... come to speak directly with the workers (*banco* owners, but sincere) of the market. You will discover many facts that you don't know (Stefano 2011).

The newspaper portrayed the city decision as a "tsunami on the market stands" (Pasquini 2011). At a subsequent City Council meeting, ambulant vendors and representatives of various political parties had an opportunity to present their views. Vendors across the marketplace huddled in groups to listen to a live broadcast of the meeting on radios. An opposition party member urged elected officials to keep in mind that some licensed owners were elderly and in poor health. They were unable to work outside any longer and had no choice but to rent their stand. If one owns a house, he pointed out, one can rent it, so why not a *banco*? Vendors listening on their radios in San Lorenzo reacted with thunderous applause. The mayor rejected the comparison, noting that a house is on private, not public, property, and urged ambulant vendors to stop "fishing in the lake of memories." Other speakers pointed out that the city had not even made much of an attempt to help the ambulant vendors succeed by simply installing signs that labeled San Lorenzo a "historic market," even though the courtesy had been given to vendors in the New Market. A motion was subsequently passed to allow a directional marker to be installed that now appears in the underground walkway connecting the train station and the area of the Santa Maria Novella Church.

In the weeks that followed, there was a rollercoaster of emotions. Beatrice worried aloud, "What are we supposed to do? We are too young to retire but too old to find other work. I am lucky; at least my children have state jobs. They have work and a place to live. What about those among us who also must provide for children?" Ennio, too, was apprehensive, saying:

> We will be ok [in our license renewal request], we follow every rule, and our record is spotless. I am sure yours is, too [in reference to Beatrice]. We pay our taxes, we never use an extra centimeter of space, I have always kept my *banco* clean and never left a mess. But the issue for me is: who

can work under controls like this? First they take away licenses; then, what will they ask of those of us who are allowed to keep ours? Will we have to buy new *banchi* that someone else thinks are more beautiful? I can't afford to do it: the new ones cost €20,000, and my old one still works fine.

In the midst of the arguments over the fate of the *banchi*, the mayor offered another proposition intended to increase the *fiorentinità* of the zone: the addition of a marble façade over the rough stone face of San Lorenzo Church. Michelangelo Buonarotti had actually created models for a planned future façade, and the proposal to affix a marble frontage was presented by the mayor as the recuperation of part of the neighborhood's material heritage. The mayor justified the proposal, explaining, "I must restore one of the most beautiful zones of Florence ... without fear that ... the power of the revenue of the *banchi* will be reduced. [I say] let's repossess ourselves of a piece of *fiorentinità*!" (Ferrara 2011: 36). He added later:

> To all the professional naysayers, I say that this city is culturally full of façades remade later, or of bridges remade later. And I think that no one can argue with the enormous communicative value and marketing that this operation would bring to Florence, that it would receive a lot of attention the world over. To the citizens I say: let's keep San Lorenzo more secure, let's put the market in order and at the end, the Florentines will decide if they vote yes or no to Michelangelo's façade; the Florentines [will decide] because the city belongs to the Florentines ... and that's the end of it! (*La Nazione* 2011b)[4]

If construction had proceeded at that time, the façade would have been completed by 2015, in time for the 150th anniversary of Florence's 1865 inauguration as the temporary capital of the new nation of Italy. The work is still under consideration and has not yet begun, however.

As the summer of 2011 unfolded, Alessandra, who had described previously relationships in the market as the "lovely side" of her work life, was anxious. "I am sick to my stomach," she told me. "There is talk that changing San Lorenzo Church will restore *fiorentinità*, but the market that we work in isn't considered important. There is no security. I am 45 and not getting younger! I can't live like this. I am going to sell my *banco*, maybe leave

---

4 The Medici Pope Leo X tasked Michelangelo Buonarotti with designing San Lorenzo's façade. Michelangelo created three-dimensional models and sketches of the proposed façade, which was, however, not completed. In 1900, the city hosted a competition to design a new facade. Ultimately the winning design could not be funded. Continued interest in the façade also motivated a 2007 event in which part of Michelangelo's original design was projected onto the front of San Lorenzo Church. Discussion of restoring the façade has also evoked some tongue-in-cheek responses; see http://firenze2059.tumblr.com/.

San Lorenzo for a while. I need to feel like I am in control of my own life."
Indeed, claims that the *fiorentinità* of the market would be restored by removing 80 vendors struck all of my key informants as absurd. In Beatrice's words,

> How can they insist that *this* market [her emphasis] has to show *fiorentinità* and do it by taking jobs away from Florentines and removing Florentines? And why does the responsibility for showing all of this *fiorentinità* fall only on vendors here? *Fiorentinità*, ok, fine, but *fiorentinità* for me means *fiorentinità* for everyone! *Beh*, where is the *fiorentinità* in the center of this city, I ask you? Don't say that San Lorenzo has to be the place of *fiorentinità* simply because the city decided to allow a Hard Rock Cafe to open in the Piazza della Repubblica! Believe me, there is nothing Florentine about a Hard Rock Cafe! At €2.50 for a coffee, how many of us could even afford to go? Show me the *fiorentinità*!

Fiorentinità and Its Discontents

> There is no greater sorrow than to recall happiness in the midst of misery.
> —Dante Alighieri

Although wrangling over issues of license renewal continued, in the end all licenses held by marketers whose taxes and fees were up to date were renewed. Planning for the market's physical reorganization continued, however. By mid-2013 there was no question that the city would require every *banco* in the immediate environs of the San Lorenzo Church to be removed (Mugnaini 2013). Owners would be given the opportunity to be relocated, mostly to the piazza behind the Central Market building, once dumpsters there were replaced by underground trash receptacles. A slew of protests and special meetings followed; many were recorded and uploaded to YouTube and other social media. On one occasion, vendors rolled *banchi* into the church's *piazza* but did not open them. Instead, they mounted signs explaining that they wanted to work but were being deprived of their livelihood. In short, they emphasized their strong work ethic and the risk that closing *banchi* posed to the survival of their families. By January 2014, however, the removal was complete. The mayor tweeted, "Today we have liberated, as promised, the San Lorenzo [Church] area, one of the most beautiful places in the world." The city immediately began excavating a broad swath of the church piazza to replace sewer pipes beneath it, while displaced vendors accused the city of "asphalting over workers."

Despite some vendors' relocation to more crowded, less visible spaces behind the market building, sporadic protests continued. At one point a group hung a banner declaring the San Lorenzo Church piazza to be the "San Lorenzo Cemetery." Rather than bringing their *banchi*, each set out a cardboard box made to look like a gravestone. "Epitaphs" were added noting how long each merchant had operated a *banco* outside the church. Meanwhile, signs that had previously been hung on buildings by shop owners who felt the presence of *banchi* negatively affected their own businesses were replaced by new ones reading "STILL WALLED IN ALIVE? NO! THANK YOU."

In April 2014, the city celebrated the reopening of the Central Market building's first floor. Jacopo's prediction that he would not be invited to return upstairs proved correct. Where he and others used to sell figs, fennel, and flowers, there is now a large sports bar, a cooking school, restaurants, and more. It is already receiving strong reviews on travel review sites. The new first-floor businesses are permitted to maintain a different operating schedule from the ground-floor establishments. The first floor is accessible to the public for more hours every day, and on seven rather than six days a week.

From their *banchi* in front of the market building, Silver Street vendors observed these developments just as they have so many others throughout the market zone. The relocation of so many *banchi* suggests to them that changes to their own allotments of space will probably follow. Having witnessed the effect that recent changes have had on the livelihoods of others, some are fearful for their own fates. Even if they are permitted to remain, they question whether the marketplace will ever be as lucrative and lively as before. For example, while some Silver Street vendors seem to be experiencing an uptick in sales that they attribute to the presence of fewer *banchi* overall, they suggest that having fewer vendors in the marketplace probably does not serve their interests in the long run. In the past, they point out, the expansiveness of the market was part of its attraction, and they maintain that, in this age of mass tourism, the city gave up an important tourism asset, and part of its *fiorentinità*, when it chose to displace vendors from the church piazza.

However others in this city may personally feel about the most recent chapters in the unfolding story of this market, everyone recognizes that the marketplace's future is inexorably linked to the fate of the historic center and therefore the stakes are high (*La Nazione* 2013). In this regard I recall my conversation with a merchant who owns a luxury-goods store a few blocks from the marketplace. I asked what he expected would happen next. His trenchant response linked San Lorenzo's latest evolution to the city's politics and economics more generally:

> Listen, the right question isn't what will happen next. The right question is who will come along next? Don't think of that building as a market. Think of it as a fortress. What did Florentines do to fortresses throughout history? Besieged them. The occupants defended themselves as best they could, consumed everything they had, surrendered, and left. There is

plenty of evidence; what about that elevator to the first floor inside the market? Now it works, but it was broken for ages. Do you really believe that in this city an elevator can't be fixed in one day? But the parts to fix that particular one never seemed to arrive. Then the first floor of the building was closed and didn't reopen for years. The point isn't that it reopened with nice wine bars or big-screen televisions. The point is that it was closed for years. Everyone wants to seize a fortress. But in Florence, we just don't always know who is leading the charge and who is defending what.

CHAPTER SIX

FIORENTINITÀ IN A POST-FLORENTINE MARKET

> It is difficult to "halt" San Lorenzo's motion. The neighborhood doesn't stay still: it is unable to. It is the historic center's port ... passageways through which half the world enters Florence, exits it, consumes it ... movements of populations ... of new things to sell and ways to sell them (Filardo and Savorelli 2008: 2).

This book has focused primarily upon the views and experiences of long-term ambulant vendors in a changing neighborhood environment. Readers who have been to Florence are likely to have seen their *banchi* or even paused to consider their merchandise. It has been my great fortune to have passed 10 field seasons among them and to have involved some of my students in the project as research assistants. Like many relationships that make up the "lovely side" of working in San Lorenzo, my relationships with my informants have also deepened over time. The merchants I know best have gradually and patiently helped me to understand the activities that their livelihood entails, how they think those tasks should be performed, the old and new challenges they must surmount to earn a living, and the passion they feel for their profession as well as for this place.

The book has also addressed how important developments related to transnational migration and globalization are transforming the face and space of a neighborhood that has long been at or near the heart of commerce in Florence. As Ted Lewellen has noted, anthropology today emphasizes "process, fluidity, agency, and overlapping and multidimensional networks" (2002: 33), due in part to its engagement with globalization and globalization literatures. In that regard, one of my undergraduate research assistants ended her field journal with the comment, "I have realized how much I will miss this market. I discovered a lot about how vendors think and how different ethnicities have different ways of interacting with each other and customers. San Lorenzo is a microcosm of the international business scene and of diversity in business. It is the whole world inside beautiful Florence."

FIGURE 6.1: San Lorenzo Night celebration, 2015.
CREDIT: Anne Schiller

Efforts to revitalize San Lorenzo clearly involve a host of stakeholders who sometimes have very different perspectives and priorities. Some of their preferences are compatible and others not. Various chapters have pointed out that rumors, hearsay, and lack of an official long-term plan for the zone have made some *sanlorenzini* very anxious. At the same time, other *sanlorenzini* believe that the neighborhood has turned a corner and, with the grand reopening of the first floor of the Central Market building and the removal of *banchi* from the area alongside the church, has already begun to recoup its reputation as a decorous and pleasant zone for residents to frequent. Practically the only constant I have encountered over the period in which I have conducted research is that a broad range of stakeholders wants something to be done about, for, or in San Lorenzo. While nearly everyone agrees that more action is needed, consensus has not been reached on exactly what it should be, or on what exactly restoration of *fiorentinità* would look like. As Jeanette Edwards suggested in her study of the heritage industry in northwest England, nostalgia alone is not enough to explain the prominence of residents' constructions of the past in their contemporary identity. Rather, as she noted, "The past presents people with a problem: what to select and what to ignore; what to emphasise and what to screen out. Stories about the past do not merely render visible a person's connections to persons and places, they make and break those connections. They constitute local identities ..." (1998: 150).

For the primary subjects of this volume, licensed Florentine or other merchants with at least a decade of experience under their belt, who pay taxes and discharge all the responsibilities that operating a registered business there entails, the predicament seems straightforward. Their way of life has become vulnerable in a city where they feel that few civic administrators seem inclined to hear them out. They address and serve a public comprising all nationalities of tourists but ever fewer neighborhood and city residents. They look around and see forms of illegal vending that further underscore how much their marketplace has changed. To survive in their environment they must compete with one another, with shops, with newcomers for whom the marketplace may simply represent a short-term economic opportunity, and with infringers. Infringers do not or cannot follow the rules, and therefore they personify, in long-term vendors' eyes, what the market was never intended to be, even if some of the current infringers might welcome the opportunity to become legal merchants and embrace local marketplace norms. Though some vendor families have worked the same spot for generations, the current generation worries that the city may rescind their licenses, or renew them only if they move to a less auspicious location—one with hardly enough space between themselves and the next vendor to unfurl their canvas awnings. City officials who would like to assist displaced vendors to remain in the market ponder arrangements and rearrangements of *banchi* as if they were moving checkers on a checkerboard.

The current and future state of San Lorenzo is also a concern for residents and shop owners. Memory, nostalgia, and longing combine for them, as they do for market vendors. When San Lorenzo was the city's pulse point, the market brought recognition and revenue to their neighborhood in ways that paralleled its Florentine ambience. Long-time residents remember a busy market and the satisfying sounds of a smaller number of merchants interacting in the streets, both with one another and with people from different neighborhoods. But today many residents feel that the marketplace has become noisy, crowded, and precarious. Some see even licensed vendors as part of the problem, reasoning that were it not for their presence, the tourists who went there would be drawn specifically by the neighborhood's remarkable art and architecture, and not because they were out hunting for bargains. Infringers selling counterfeit designer purses and pirated compact discs would stay away because there would be fewer tourists and thus fewer clients. Streets would once again be navigable, storefronts would be visible, the morning wake-up call of hundreds of *banchi* being wheeled across paving stones would end, and the streets would not be as littered. Different stakeholders clearly espouse different views about what it means to preserve this market, its heritage, and Florence's commercial tradition.

At several points in this book San Lorenzo has been referred to as a neighborhood on the move. Regardless of why some people migrate out

FIGURE 6.2: Portrait of a Central Market fruit vendor. The painting is entitled "Purple Flower."
CREDIT: Oil Painting by Steve Kalar

of San Lorenzo or spend money elsewhere, it is undeniable that the types
of goods and services offered by many businesses surrounding the marketplace are different from before. As the ranks of native Florentine-owned
enterprises within and close to the market dwindle, immigrant-owned

FIGURE 6.3: Anonymous signage: "Let's save San Lorenzo."
CREDIT: Anne Schiller

businesses burgeon. Stakeholders continue to try to raise awareness and resources for neighborhood improvement that may staunch outmigration and enhance viability for old-timers and newcomers alike. The Lorenzo de' Medici Institute, for example, once hosted an exhibition inside the Central Market that featured a "San Lorenzo Survival Kit." Conceived partly in farcical spirit but intended to bring positive attention to this landmark, the kit included a Renaissance-inspired gown with pockets large enough to hold groceries. The gown could be transformed into a tent that provided outdoor shelter in inclement weather while the wearer was waiting for the authorities to open the Central Market's doors. The kit also included a cart that could be converted into a seat if the climb up the Market's interior staircase to the first floor proved too daunting to be ascended without taking a rest (given that the elevator was so often broken). A poem that addressed the marketplace's survival was also included in the exhibition. Modeled after the conjugation of present-tense Italian verbs, it was perhaps also an *hommage* to foreigners who come to Florence to learn the beautiful Italian language and to immigrants who arrive there in search of a better life:

> i survive you survive she survives he survives
> it survives we survive you survive they survive
> san lorenzo survives the young survives
> the old survives the ideas survive the culture survives
> the dog survives the cat survives the italian survives
> the stranger survives the tourist survives
> san lorenzo survives the butcher survives
> the baker survives the greengrocer survives
> the student survives the art survives i survive
> you survive she survives he survives it survives
> we survive you survive they survive san lorenzo survives
> firenze lives.
>
> (Ghielmetti 2007)

This book has suggested that long-term vendors like Silvio, Ivana, Beatrice, Dante, George, Niccolò, Ennio, Jacopo, Alessandra, Akka, Eva, and their neighbors, all survivors in their own way, are well accustomed to adapting to change. As resourceful businessmen and businesswomen, they seized new opportunities such as the relaxation of redundancy rules and made the most of the occasion. Changes such as an increase in fees were accepted with resignation because at least their marketplace had remained intact, infused with traditions and a robust set of social norms. As long as they could make a fair living, enjoy their independence, and relish their relationships with customers and other vendors, they wanted to stay.

In Chapter Three I quoted Alessandra, who said to me, "If you felt what I am feeling, you wouldn't have to ask me why I have worked here my whole life." Even after 10 field seasons, I cannot possibly claim to feel precisely what she experiences. Still, thanks to informants who shared their lives with me and to the discipline of anthropology, which taught me that diligence, attentiveness, sensitivity, and patience are among the fundamental requirements of participant-observation fieldwork, I have more than an inkling of what Alessandra meant. Returning day after day and year after year gave me the opportunity to witness and be part of interactions that, over time, enabled me to recognize the affective dimensions of interpersonal interactions in the marketplace and helped me understand what it feels like to be a long-term San Lorenzo vendor. I recall in this regard a client from Minnesota whom Ivana and I assisted in 2011. Transfixed by a display of resin angels hanging from invisible threads at the front of the *banco*, the woman told us that she had two young granddaughters who had just lost their father, her son, after a long illness. Her eyes filled with tears and she said, "I want to buy two beautiful angels, one for each of my girls. Those angels will be what my granddaughters remember me by when I am also gone. As they get older, they will see them and know that I loved them." The price for the pair of angels, €36, took her momentarily aback. But the client did not ask for a discount. Rather, she replied, "Well, for me that's a lot of money. But my friend went to Germany and bought her grandchildren stuffed animals. They played with them for thirty seconds and then forgot about them. I don't want to be forgotten." Ivana embraced the woman tightly, pressed a smaller but equally lovely third angel in her hand as a gift, and then patted her arm. I think I understood how Ivana was experiencing that moment. So, while I can't be sure that Alessandra was correct when she told me, "You can't get this feeling anywhere but San Lorenzo," I do know that it was lovely.

Lately, however, with the realization that some people in this city seemingly do not consider ambulant vending particularly important to preserve, the specter of the marketplace's demise or transformation into a very different entity has seemed formidable enough to be genuinely intimidating to my informants. Vendors cite examples of what they perceive as disregard for their contributions to the tax base and their value as part of the heritage of this city of merchants. Recall that only a few years ago the area around the San Lorenzo Church was described as the neighborhood's "commercial entrance." Now, after more than half a millennium, the days of robust ambulant vending there have apparently drawn to a close.

As far as my informants are concerned, uncertainty is troubling. They explain that they need more information to make a determination about their future. They ask themselves if they should try to move to another part of the city or even rent a shop. They wonder whether to invest in a new *banco* when their licenses could be revoked or their businesses relocated. Their situation speaks to an issue raised in Chapter Three: for San Lorenzo vendors, like vendors everywhere, information is vital. In its absence, they cannot compete successfully. These marketplace men and women, who have always prided themselves on their independence, do not like to feel that they are at the mercy of others who seem to have very different views about what constitutes *fiorentinità* or simply the appropriate use of public space.

At the time of writing, the façade of the San Lorenzo Church remains rough-hewn as Michelangelo left it, unembellished by marble.

FIGURE 6.4: San Lorenzo church façade decorated with a banner depicting the martyred saint.
CREDIT: Anne Schiller

Notwithstanding numerous assemblies, press conferences, and grassroots efforts, the future of the marketplace continues to be under discussion. Some produce vendors, like Jacopo who used to work alongside his grandfather at this market, have relocated operations to available slots on the ground floor of the Central Market building. Many other produce vendors left San Lorenzo after the tent behind the market, where they had worked for years during the first floor's renovation, was dismantled. Alessandra and GianLuca closed their *banco* in 2012. That same year, George and Evan faced the fact that their family bread business could no longer support them both. Evan left to search for other opportunities, and George now tries his best by himself to serve both the customers inside the Central Market and his outdoor vendor clientele. When the first floor of the Central Market finally reopened in 2014, my key informants did not rush to visit, but now they occasionally stop in to catch a moment of *Fiorentina* matches on the widescreen televisions before having to hurry back to their *banchi*.

Throughout the clamor that has surrounded developments in the market zone, tangible and intangible dimensions of *fiorentinità* are ever more explicitly drawn into debate. For instance, while not all vendors and residents are in favor of spending money on a new church façade, many agree that its installation could increase *fiorentinità* in an appropriate way. Their arguments recall earlier ones concerning how the mysterious disappearance of the serpentine portico behind the market building diminished the market's *fiorentinità*. Some residents claim that if the Central Market ground floor were also restored in an "authentic" way, with less emphasis on *turistica* and more on well-priced staples, locals might return. The tourists who do go there seeking authentic cultural experiences would be presented with new opportunities to shop in the Italian style and to experience concentrated *fiorentinità* firsthand.

If San Lorenzo must be redirected from what it has become, what should that direction be? There are those who already consider the market to be unrecognizable. But conversations about the future have brought neither consensus nor concord. I have shown that many there believe that "cultural restoration" in some form is a priority (*La Nazione* 2011a). But I have also noted that not everyone agrees that *fiorentinità* should or even can be its defining characteristic. As a former officer of "Together for San Lorenzo" remarked to me, "I am tired of hearing about *fiorentinità*. I am Florentine, but Florence isn't a museum. This neighborhood isn't a museum, either, and anyone who wants to see '*Firenze come'ra*' ['Florence as it was'] should go to the topographical museum on dell'Oriuolo Street. *Sanlorenzini* want to be progressive and live and work in a progressive neighborhood. Our identity is multicultural. That is who we are, and that is what we have to nurture." In 2012, to help dissipate rising tensions, a motivated group of residents and vendors organized an open-air dinner in the church square "to remember who we are" and "to express who we will be" (Baldi 2012a; 2012b). The theme of that 2012 communal dinner was "There Is San Lorenzo: Residents, Ambulant Vendors, Shop Owners, and Workers All Together," emphatically underscoring that San Lorenzo is vital and real. More recently, tensions among some residents and some vendors threatened to cast a pall over the 2014 San Lorenzo Night celebration. Still, the event went on as planned, with volunteers organized by the Natural Commercial Center Association, a group of local businessmen and businesswomen, cooking 440 pounds of spaghetti sauce while the San Lorenzo Market Consortium, another neighborhood improvement organization founded by vendors, some residents, and some shop owners, brought in over 4,000 pounds of watermelon (Gori 2014).

San Lorenzo thus remains, for now, a neighborhood with both an identity and an identity crisis, much like some of the people associated with it. The case of San Lorenzo, then, allows us better to understand the evolution of personal and collective identities, the exercise of different forms of power, and how heritage may be created, maintained, or transformed. For all of these reasons, and others besides, what is happening in San Lorenzo will continue to be of interest in Florence, throughout Italy and Europe, and beyond, and not only to those of us who profoundly admire this city. In years to come, the political, social, cultural, and economic consequences of San Lorenzo's transformation will continue to be discussed by residents, merchants, scholars, and others drawn to this celebrated city. How *fiorentinità* figures in the ongoing evolution of this zone, and how it may or may not correspond to sociocultural change there, will be questioned as well.

For example, in an article entitled "Florence with Almond Eyes," a local newspaper reported that growing numbers of Florentines frequent businesses owned by immigrants or first-generation Italians. By way of example, it described the "surprising" arrival at an immigrant-owned hair salon of "Fernanda, the 'Florentinest' of clients." The article concluded that while generations must pass before the city achieves "true integration," the requirements of that integration "seem to be in place" (*Il Nuovo Corriere di Firenze* 2010). For me, the article called to mind a conversation that I had a few years earlier with another local resident, in which I asked what *fiorentinità* meant to her. Her response was illuminating:

> You know that park at the end of Faenza Street, near the Fortezza da Basso? There you can see *fiorentinità*. It's a monument and that isn't its real name, but everyone knows it is the monument of *fiorentinità*.[1] I remember someone even asking me if I had seen "the *fiorentinità*," so that's what it is. When they began building this monument it looked like a staircase, and I really liked it. Stairs are very evocative. Here, in Italy, people gather on stairways to talk; they go up and down steps to church; they sit outdoors on stairs to read a book; [stairs are] public and lively. Just look at the way people like to sit on the steps of the San Lorenzo Church. But then they suddenly started putting statues on the top. Dante and all the rest of them, even the actor [Roberto] Benigni. It was crowded with public figures, most of them dead. No room left up there. Then, can you

---

1 For a photograph of the monument by Mario Ceroli, see http://www.marioceroli.it/Opere/ Installazioni/7/SILENZIO-ASCOLTATE/1661/ . The monument is named "Silenzio: ascoltate!" and was commissioned as part of the 2007 Florentine Genius Project.

believe it, they cordoned it off with a rope! And I realized, as I stood looking at it, that the first step was too high to be a real step anyway. That's
fiorentinità, you understand? It is something you can't get to anymore.

Fiorentinità, then, is an attribute that can be seen, heard, touched, and tasted,
but it is also defunct, gone missing, and aspirational all at the same time.
It may or may not be a new façade on an old church, a spirited exchange
between a tourist-shopper and an ambulant vendor, a seemingly friendly
greeting between two merchants setting up their *banchi* side by side on a
noisy street, or even a joke about current events. *Fiorentinità* is both as real
and as ephemeral as a marketplace that pulsates like a beating heart in the
daylight but then vanishes at night. As such, it is reminiscent of the falling
stars one may glimpse on August 10, San Lorenzo Night, when the neighbourhood honors its patron saint. It is on these stars that *sanlorenzini* make
their wishes. As this volume has explained, what some of them wish for is
as simple as the chance to continue enjoying the "lovely side" of their lives
from what is, for now, a precarious perch on bumpy asphalt in the heart of
one of the most beautiful cities in the world.

BIBLIOGRAPHY

Agostini, Amadore. 2007. "Far West in San Lorenzo. E´ Guerra al Mercato. Ambulanti e Abusivi, Convivenza Impossibile." *La Nazione* 23 May: 5.

Ahmad, Yahaya. 2006. "The Scope and Definitions of Heritage: From Tangible to Intangible." *International Journal of Heritage Studies* 12 (3): 292–300. http://dx.doi.org/10.1080/13527250600604639.

Akerlof, George, and Rachel Kranton. 2010. *Identity Economics: How Our Identities Shape Our Work, Wages, and Well-Being.* Princeton, NJ: Princeton University Press.

Albahari, Maurizio. 2010. "Al confine della primavera." *Italian Culture* 28 (2): 82–84. http://dx.doi.org/10.1179/016146210X12790095562986.

Associazione Insieme Per San Lorenzo. n.d. *Contributo alla Discussione sul Riassetto del Mercato Esterno di San Lorenzo.* Unpublished Manuscript.

Babb, Florence. 1989. *Between Field and Cooking Pot: The Political Economy of Marketwomen in Peru.* Austin: University of Texas Press.

Baldi, Emanuele. 2009. "Multe Solo Agli Ambulanti. É Rivolta Contro Gli Abusivi. Banchi Ingombranti, Maxi Multa." *Il Firenze* 9 July: 23.

Baldi, Emanuele. 2012a. "Il Sorriso di San Lorenzo." *La Nazione* 7 June: 1.

Baldi, Emanuele. 2012b. "L'Orgoglio di San Lorenzo." *La Nazione* 9 June: 17.

Barbagli, Marzio, and Laura Sartori. 2004. "Law Enforcement Activities in Italy." *Journal of Modern Italian Studies* 9 (2): 161–85. http://dx.doi.org/10.1080/13545710410001679457.

Barth, Fredrik. (Original work published 1969) 1998. *Ethnic Groups and Boundaries. Reissued edition.* Prospect Heights, IL: Waveland Press.

Belmonte, Thomas. 1989. *The Broken Fountain.* Second Expanded Edition. New York: Columbia University Press.

Bencistà, Alessandro. 2001. *Vocabolario del Vernacolo Fiorentino.* Firenze: Libreria Chiari.

Bestor, Theodore. 2004. *Tsukiji: The Fish Market at the Center of the World.* Berkeley: University of California Press.

Bianca, Mariano. 1995. *I Mercati Nella Storia di Firenze.* Firenze: Loggia de' Lanzi.

Bigot, Giulia, and Stefano Fella. 2008. "The Prodi Government's Proposed Citizenship Reform, and the Debate on Immigration and Its Impact in Italy." *Modern Italy* 13 (3): 305–15. http://dx.doi.org/10.1080/13532940802185097.

Black, Rachel. 2012. *Porta Palazzo: The Anthropology of an Italian Market.* Philadelphia: University of Pennsylvania Press. http://dx.doi.org/10.9783/9780812205794.

Bonanni, Giuseppina. 2013. *Migranti—Le Cifre 2013. A Cura di Giuseppina Bonanni.* Firenze: Comune di Firenze.

Bourdieu, Pierre. 1977. *Outline of a Theory of Practice.* Trans. Richard Nice. Cambridge: Cambridge University Press. http://dx.doi.org/10.1017/CBO9780511812507.

Breathnach, Teresa. 2006. "Looking for the Real Me: Locating the Self in Heritage Tourism." *Journal of Heritage Tourism* 1 (2): 100–120. http://dx.doi.org/10.2167/jht009.0.

Brochmann, Grete. 1996. *European Integration and Immigration from Third Countries.* Oslo: Scandinavian University Press.

Bromley, Ray. 2013. "Rethinking the Public Realm: On Vending, Popular Protest, and Street Politics." In *Street Economies in the Urban Global South*, ed. Karen Hansen, Walter Little, and B. Lynne Milgram, 17–28. Santa Fe: School for Advanced Research Press.

Brown, Dan. 2003. *The Da Vinci Code.* New York: Doubleday.

Brucker, Gene, ed. 1967. *Two Memoirs of Renaissance Florence: The Diaries of Buonaccorso Pitti and Gregorio Dati.* Trans. Julia Martines. New York: Harper & Row.

Brucker, Gene. 1983. *Renaissance Florence.* Berkeley: University of California Press.

Bruner, Edward. 1966. Review of *Peddlers and Princes: Social Change and Economic Modernization in Two Indonesian Towns*, by Clifford Geertz. *American Anthropologist* 68 (1): 255–58. http://dx.doi.org/10.1525/aa.1966.68.1.02a00570.

Bryceson, Deborah, Judith Okely, and Jonathan Webber, eds. 2007. *Identity and Networks. Fashioning Gender and Ethnicity across Cultures.* Oxford: Berghahn Books.

Chiarini, Gloria. 2004. *A Spasso per San Lorenzo. Storie e Scenari nel Quartiere Mediceo.* Firenze: Mega Review Srl.

Ciabani, Roberto. 1994. *Le Potenze di Firenze: Una Pagina Inedita di Storia Fiorentina.* Firenze: Bonechi.

Ciabani, Roberto. 1998. *Firenze: Di Gonfalone in Gonfalone.* Firenze: Edizioni della Meridiana.

Clemente, Pietro. 2010. "Negoziare le Diversitá: La Vita Quotidiana Come Patrimonio Culturale." In *Cittá e Mercati*, ed. Lucia Schianchi, 20–35. Parma: graficheSTEPeditrice.

Cole, Jeffrey. 1997. *The New Racism in Europe: A Sicilian Ethnography.* Cambridge: Cambridge University Press. http://dx.doi.org/10.1017/CBO9780511520952.

Colombo, Asher, and Giuseppe Scortino. 2004. Italian Immigration: The Origins, Nature, and Evolution of Italy's Migratory Systems. *Journal of Modern Italian Studies* 9(1): 49–70.

Comaroff, John, and Jean Comaroff. 2009. *Ethnicity, Inc.* Chicago: University of Chicago Press. http://dx.doi.org/10.7208/chicago/9780226114736.001.0001.

Conte, Rossella. 2014. "Capo, È'Nuovo di Zecca: Facciamo 40 Euro. San Lorenzo, Il Mercato Nero Delle Bici Rubate." *La Nazione* 30 May: 1.

Corbetta, Guido. 1995. "Patterns of Development of Family Businesses in Italy." *Family Business Review* 8 (4): 255–65. http://dx.doi.org/10.1111/j.1741-6248.1995.00255.x.

Corriere Fiorentino. 2010. "Blitz Degli Ambulanti in San Lorenzo." 17 March: 1.

Counihan, Carole. 2004. *Around the Tuscan Table: Food, Family, and Gender in Twentieth-Century Florence.* New York: Routledge.

Dati, Gregorio. 1902. *Storia di Firenze di Gregorio Dati dal 1380 al 1405. A cura di Luigi Pratesi.* Perugia: Norcia.

De Vos, George. 2006. "Introduction: Ethnic Pluralism: Conflict and Accommodation." In *Ethnic Identity. Problems and Prospects for the Twenty-First Century*, ed. Lola Romanucci-Ross, George De Vos, and Takeyuki Tsuda, 1–35. Lanham, MD: AltaMira Press.

De Vos, George, and Lola Romanucci-Ross. 2006. "Conclusion: Ethnic Identity: A Psychocultural Perspective." In *Ethnic Identity. Problems and Prospects for the Twenty-First Century*, ed. Lola Romanucci-Ross, George De Vos, and Takeyuki Tsuda, 375–400. Lanham, MD: AltaMira Press.

DeWalt, Kathleen, and Billie DeWalt. 2011. *Participant Observation: A Guide for Fieldworkers.* Lanham, MD: AltaMira Press.

Di Giovine, Michael. 2009. *The Heritage-scape: UNESCO, World Heritage, and Tourism.* Lanham, MD: Lexington Books.

Diani, Mario. 2004. "Networks and Participation." In *The Blackwell Companion to Social Movements*, ed. David Snow, Sarah Soule, and Hanspeter Kriesi, 339–59. Oxford: Blackwell.

DiMaggio, Paul. 1994. "Culture and Economy." In *The Handbook of Economic Sociology*, ed. Neil Smelser and Richard Swedberg, 27–57. Princeton, NJ: Princeton University Press.

Eckstein, Nicholas. 2006. "Neighborhood as Microcosm." In *Renaissance Florence. A Social History*, ed. Roger Crum and John T. Paoletti, 219–239. New York: Cambridge University Press.

Edwards, Jeanette. 1998. "The Need for 'a Bit of History': Place and Past in English Identity." In *Locality and Belonging*, ed. Nadia Lovell, 147–67. London: Routledge.

Faesani, Francesco. 2009. *Undocumented Migration: Counting the Uncountable. Data and Trends across Europe*. Bremen: European Union.

Fallaci, Oriana. 2002. *The Rage and the Pride*. New York: Rizzoli.

Ferrara, Ernesto. 2011. "Firenze 'Completiamo la Basilica di Michelangelo.'" *La Nazione* 26 July: 36.

Filardo, Daria, and Alessandro Savorelli. 2008. *San Lorenzo: Un Quartiere in Movimento*. Ideazione e Gestione Progetto Martino Marangoni. Firenze: Polistampa.

Il Firenze. 2009. "San Lorenzo, Ci Risiamo Abusivi all'Assalto di Touristi." 9 July: 22.

Frantz, David. 2003. *Lorenzo Market between Diversity and Mutation. Note di Lavoro 69*. Milan: Fondazione Eni Enrico Mattei.

García y Griego, Manuel. 1992. "Canada: Flexibility and Control in Immigration and Refugee Policy." In *Controlling Immigration: A Global Perspective*, ed. Wayne Cornelius, Philip Martin, and James Hollifield, 119–40. Stanford, CA: Stanford University Press.

Geertz, Clifford. 1963. *Peddlers and Princes: Social Change and Economic Development in Two Indonesian Towns*. Chicago: University of Chicago Press.

Geertz, Clifford. 1978. "The Bazaar Economy: Information and Search in Peasant Marketing." *American Economic Review* 68 (2): 28–32.

Ghielmetti, Paolo. 2007. *San Lorenzo Survives*. http://it.groups.yahoo.com/group/Succedeafirenze/message/905?i.

Giannelli, Luca. 2007. *Firenze Popolare*. Firenze: Scramasax.

Gianni, Laura. 2013. "Spintoni e minacce, a un passo dalla rissa, Commercianti-vu'comfra' ai ferri corti." *La Nazione* 23 July: 3.

Goffman, Erving. 1959. *The Presentation of Self in Everyday Life*. Garden City, NJ: Doubleday.

Goffman, Erving. 1971. *Relations in Public: Microstudies of the Public Order*. New York: Basic Books.

Goode, Erich, and Nachman Ben-Yehuda. 1994. *Moral Panics: The Social Construction of Deviance*. Oxford, Cambridge: Blackwell.

Gordon, Christina, and Gunasehare Shunmugamm. 2007. "Immigrant Vendors and Social Change in an 'Italian' Market: The Case of San Lorenzo." *North Carolina State University Undergraduate Research Journal* 3: 27–33.

Gori, Giulio. 2014. "San Lorenzo, 200 chili di ragù per battere le tensioni." *Corriere Fiorentino* 6 August. http://corrierefiorentino.corriere.it/firenze/notizie/cronaca/2014/6-agosto-2014/san-lorenzo-200-chili-ragu-battere-tensioni-223697106830.shtml.

Gori, Giulio. 2015. "Sant'Orsola riapre, con le opera d'arte." *Corriere Fiorentino* 3 October.

Grillo, Ralph, and Jeff Pratt, eds. 2002. *The Politics of Recognizing Difference: Multiculturalism Italian Style*. Aldershot, UK: Ashgate.

Hammersley, Martyn, and Paul Atkinson. 2007. *Ethnography: Principles in Practice*. 3rd ed. London: Routledge.

Harrison, Rodney, ed. 2010. *Understanding the Politics of Heritage*. Manchester: University of Manchester Press.

Herzfeld, Michael. 2004. *The Body Impolitic: Artisans and Artifice in the Global Hierarchy of Value*. Chicago: University of Chicago Press.

Herzfeld, Michael. 2009. *Evicted from Eternity. The Restructuring of Modern Rome*. Chicago: University of Chicago Press. http://dx.doi.org/10.7208/chicago/9780226329079.001.0001.

Hibbert, Christopher. 2004. *Florence. The Biography of a City*. London: Penguin Books.

Hollifield, James, Philip Martin, and Pia Orrenius, eds. 2014. *Controlling Immigration: A Global Perspective*. 3rd ed. Stanford, CA: Stanford University Press.

Horner, Susan, and Joanna Horner. 1877. *Walks in Florence: Churches, Streets and Palaces*. London: Henry S. King & Co.

Howard, Peter. 2003. *Heritage: Management, Interpretation, Identity*. London: Continuum.

Hunt, Jocelyn. 1999. *The Renaissance*. London: Routledge.

Jarves, James. 1881. "The Ideal Florentine: A Life Story Full of Life Lessons for Merchant Princes." *New York Times* 30 October.

Jenkins, Richard. 2014. *Social Identity*. 4th ed. London: Routledge.

Kent, D., and F. Kent. 1982. *Neighbours and Neighbourhood in Renaissance Florence: The District of the Red Lion in the Fifteenth Century*. Locust Valley, NY: J.J. Augustin.

Kenyon, Frederic, ed. 1899. *The Letters of Elizabeth Barrett Browning*. New York: The Macmillan Company.

Kertzer, David. 1980. *Comrades and Christians. Religion and Political Struggle in Communist Italy.* Cambridge: Cambridge University Press.

Khouma, Pap. 2010. *I Was An Elephant Salesman: Adventures between Dakar, Paris, and Milan.* Ed. Oreste Piavetta. Trans. Rebecca Hopkins. Introduction by Graziella Parati. Bloomington: Indiana University Press.

King, Russell. 1993. "Recent Immigration to Italy: Character, Causes, and Consequences." *GeoJournal* 30 (3): 283–92. http://dx.doi.org/10.1007/BF00806719.

King, Russell, and Jacqueline Andall. 1999. "The Geography and Economic Sociology of Recent Immigration to Italy." *Modern Italy* 4 (2): 135–58. http://dx.doi.org/10.1080/13532949908454826.

Krause, Elizabeth. 2005. *A Crisis of Births: Population Politics and Family-Making in Italy.* Belmont, CA: Wadsworth.

Kreps, Christina. 2005. "Indigenous Curation as Intangible Cultural Heritage: Thoughts on the Relevance of the 2003 UNESCO Convention." *Theorizing Cultural Heritage* 1 (2): 3–8.

Lelli, Silvia. 2010. "Il Mercato Di S. Ambrogio e Il Mercato Delle Pulci a Firenze: Trasferimenti di Mercati, Costruzione Sociale, Partecipazione Spontanea e Organizzata." In *Città e Mercati*, ed. Lucia Schianchi, 110–27. Parma: graficheSTEPeditrice.

Lewellen, Ted. 2002. *The Anthropology of Globalization: Cultural Anthropology Enters the 21st Century.* Westport, CT: Bergen & Garvey.

Little, Walter. 2004. *Mayas in the Marketplace. Tourism, Globalization, and Cultural Identity.* Austin: University of Texas Press.

Lovell, Nadia. 1998. "Introduction: Belonging in Need of Emplacement?" In *Locality and Belonging*, ed. Nadia Lovell, 1–24. London: Routledge.

Lucht, Hans. 2012. *Darkness Before Daylight. African Immigrants Living on the Margins in Southern Italy Today.* Berkeley: University of California Press.

Lyon, Sarah, and E. Christian Wells. 2012. *Global Tourism: Cultural Heritage and Economic Encounters.* Ed. Sarah Lyon and E. Christian Wells. Lanham, MD: AltaMira Press.

Macdonald, Sharon, ed. 1993. *Inside European Identities: Ethnography in Western Europe.* Providence, RI: Berg.

Magatti, Mauro, and Fabio Quassoli. 2003. "Italy: Between Legal Barriers and Informal Arrangements." In *Immigrant Entrepreneurs: Venturing Abroad in the Age of Globalization*, ed. Robert Kloosterman and Jan Rath, 147–71. Oxford: Berg.

Marchini, Giampaolo. 2011. "Centro e San Lorenzo, Banchi Dimezzati. Ecco Il Piano." *La Nazione* 13 July: 2–3.

Mazzoni, Riccardo. 2006. *Grazie Oriana. Pensieri e Parole Inediti Dopo L'11 Settembre.* Firenze: Il Giornale.

Metropoli. 2006. "Fuga da San Lorenzo." 30 June: 10.

Meyrowitz, Joshua. 1990. "Redefining the Situation: Extending Dramaturgy into a Theory of Social Change and Media Effects." In *Beyond Goffman. Studies on Communication, Institution, and Social Interaction*, ed. Stephen Riggings, 65–97. Berlin: Mouton de Gruyter. http://dx.doi.org/10.1515/9783110847291.65.

Migliore, Sam. 1997. *Mal'uocchiu: Ambiguity, Evil Eye, and the Language of Distress.* Toronto: University of Toronto Press.

Miller, James. 2002. *Politics in a Museum: Governing Postwar Florence.* Westport, CT: Praeger.

Mugnaini, Olga. 2013. "Sfrattati Cinque Banchi e Un Chiosco. Scatta la "Liberazione" di San Lorenzo." *La Nazione* 25 July: 9.

La Nazione. 2006. "Invasione di Abusivi." 26 June: 23.

La Nazione. 2008. "San Lorenzo in Mani agli Abusivi. Turista Canadese Ferita, I Commercianti: "Controlli Ci Sono, Ma Loro Sono Piú Aggressivi."" 6 June: 2.

La Nazione. 2010. "Nuova Vita a Sant'Orsola; Porte Aperte alla Città." 19 October. http://www.lanazione.it/firenze/cronaca/2010/10/19/402000-nuova_vita_sant_orsola.shtml.

La Nazione. 2011a. "Polveriera San Lorenzo. Maxi Controlli Anti Degrado. San Lorenzo, Un Quartiere che Ha Bisogno di Ritrovare la Sua Identità." 4 April: 1.

La Nazione. 2011b. "La Citta' èDei Fiorentini, Non Delle Soprintendenze. Renzi Rilancia il Referendum: "Decideranno i Cittadini." 29 July: 8.

La Nazione. 2013. "Tempi Certi e Cantieri Veloci San Lorenzo Vuole Risposte Sulla Destinazione Banchi." 30 July: 11.

Il Nuovo Corriere di Firenze. 2010. "Firenze Con Gli Occhi a Mandorla." 2 August: 3.

Organisation for Economic Co-operation and Development (OECD). 2015. "Is This Humanitarian Migration Crisis Different?" *Migration Policy Debates 7*. http://www.oecd.org/migration/Is-this-refugee-crisis-different.pdf.

Parati, Graziella. 2005. *Migration Italy: The Art of Talking Back in a Destination Culture*. Toronto: University of Toronto Press.

Pardo, Italo. 1996. *Managing Existence in Naples: Morality, Action, Structure*. Cambridge: Cambridge University Press. http://dx.doi.org/10.1017/CBO9780511621802.

Parkin, David. 1998. "Foreword." In *Locality and Belonging*, ed. Nadia Lovell, ix–xiv. London: Routledge.

Pasquini, Silvia. 2011. "Tsunami Sulle Bancarelle." *La Nazione* 12 July: 5.

Pellow, Deborah, ed. 1996. *Setting Boundaries. The Anthropology of Spatial and Social Organization*. Westport, CT: Bergin & Garvey.

Pine, Jason. 2012. *The Art of Making Do in Naples*. Minneapolis: University of Minnesota Press.

Plastina, Manuela. 2005. "La Rivolta di San Lorenzo. Il Quartiere Scende in Strada. Tensione con Gli Abusivi." *La Nazione* 27 May: 7.

Prajda, Katalin. 2010. "The Florentine Scolari Family at the Court of Sigismund of Luxemburg in Buda." *Journal of Early Modern History* 14 (6): 513–33. http://dx.doi.org/10.1163/157006510X540763.

Pratolini, Vasco. 1960. *The Naked Streets*. [orig. *Il Quartiere*]. Trans. Peter and Pamela Duncan. London: Harbough.

Pratolini, Vasco. 1968. *Metello*. Trans. Raymond Rosenthal. Boston: Little, Brown and Company.

Rabo, Annika. 2005. *A Shop of One's Own. Independence and Reputation among Traders in Aleppo*. London: I.B. Tauris.

Ressa, Stefania. 2011. "Proposta Choc Per La Basilica di San Lorenzo." *Il Nuovo Corriere di Firenze* 27 July: 1–2.

Romanucci-Ross, Lola. 2006. "Matricies of an Italian Identity: Past as Prologue." In *Ethnic Identity. Problems and Prospects for the Twenty-First Century*, ed. Lola Romanucci-Ross, George De Vos, and Takeyuki Tsuda, 43–71. Lanham, MD: AltaMira Press.

Rosenthal, David. 2006. "The Spaces of Plebian Ritual and the Boundaries of Transgression." In *Renaissance Florence. A Social History*, ed. Roger J. Crum and John T. Paoletti 161–81. New York: Cambridge University Press.

Samuels, Kathryn. 2014. "What Is Cultural Heritage? Mapping a Concept, Integrating Fields." *Anthropology News* 31 (March).

SBS. 2015. "Italy Rescues 970 Migrants Abandoned by People Smugglers." 1 January. http://www.sbs.com.au/news/article/2014/12/30/italy-rescues-970-migrants-abandoned-people-smugglers.

Schiller, Anne. 1997. *Small Sacrifices: Religious Change and Cultural Identity among the Ngaju of Indonesia*. New York: Oxford University Press.

Schiller, Anne. 2001. "Talking Heads: Capturing Dayak Deathways on Film." *American Ethnologist* 28 (1): 32–55. http://dx.doi.org/10.1525/ae.2001.28.1.32.

Schiller, Anne. 2007. "Activism and Identities in an East Kalimantan Dayak Organization." *Journal of Asian Studies* 66 (1): 63–95. http://dx.doi.org/10.1017/S002191180700006X.

Schiller, Anne. 2008. "Heritage and Perceptions of Ethnicity in an 'Italian' Market: The Case of San Lorenzo." *Journal of Heritage Tourism* 3 (4): 277–88. http://dx.doi.org/10.1080/17438730802366573.

Schiller, Anne, and Christina Gordon. 2007. "The Role of Ethnic Stereotyping in a Florentine Marketplace." Poster presented at the Annual Meeting of the American Anthropological Association, Washington, DC, 28 November–2 December.

Schiller, Anne, and Daniel Shattuck. 2011. "The Embodiment of Cultural Capital in a Historic Italian Market." *Global Studies Journal* 3 (4): 1–10.

Sciortino, Giuseppe, and Asher Colombo. 2004. "The Flows and the Flood: The Public Discourse on Immigration in Italy, 1969–2001." *Journal of Modern Italian Studies* 9 (1): 94–113. http://dx.doi.org/10.1080/1354571042000179209.

Seligmann, Linda. 2004. *Peruvian Street Lives. Culture, Power, and Economy among Market Women of Cuzco*. Urbana: University of Illinois Press.

Sieni, Stefano. 1995. *I Segreti di Firenze*. Firenze: Le Lettere.

Smith, Harriet, ed. 2010. *The Autobiography of Mark Twain*. Berkeley: University of California Press.

Snow, David, and Doug McAdam. 2000. "Identity Work Processes in the Context of Social Movements: Clarifying the Identity/Movement Nexus." In *Self, Identity, and Social Movements*, ed. Sheldon Stryker, Timothy Owens, and Robert White, 41–67. Minneapolis: University of Minnesota Press.

Stacul, Jaro. 2003. *The Bounded Field. Localism and Local Identity in an Italian Alpine Valley*. New York: Berghahn Books.

Staley, Edgcumbe. 1906. *The Guilds of Florence*. London: Methuen & Co.

Stefano. 2011. "Lettera Aperta Al Sindaco 'Ascolta Noi Barocciai.'" *La Nazione* 15 July: 22.

Steger, Manfred. 2013. *Globalization: A Very Short Introduction*. 3rd ed. Oxford: Oxford University Press. http://dx.doi.org/10.1093/actrade/9780199662661.001.0001.

Stryker, Sheldon, Timothy Owens, and Robert White, eds. 2000. *Self, Identity, and Social Movements*. Minneapolis: University of Minnesota Press.

Tabegna, Laura. 2015. "La Toscana Dei Misteri. Sorpresa Nel Convento di Sant'Orsola." *La Nazione* 25 September: 19.

Throsby, David. 2003. "Cultural Capital." In *A Handbook of Cultural Economics*, ed. Ruth Towse, 166–69. Cheltenham, UK: Edward Elgar Publishing.

Tragaki, Alexandra, and Antonios Rovolis. 2014. "Immigrant Population in Italy During the First Decade of the 21st Century: Changing Demographics and Modified Settlement Patterns." *European Urban and Regional Studies* 21 (3): 286–300. http://dx.doi.org/10.1177/0969776412445829.

Turner, Victor. 1960. "Ritual Aspects of Conflict Control in African Micropolitics." In *Political Anthropology*, ed. Marc Swaartz, Victor Turner, and Arthur Tuden, 239–46. Chicago: Aldine.

Valente, Lavinia. 2003. *L'Antico Mercato delle Erbe a Livorno: Un'analisi Storico-antropologica*. MA thesis, University of Pisa.

Vallet, Elisabeth, ed. 2014. *Borders, Fences and Walls: a State of Insecurity?* Farnham, UK: Ashgate.

Vanni, Massimo. 2007. "La Provincia Vuole Comprare S. Orsola." *La Repubblica* 18 May: 1.

Vanni, Massimo. 2013. "Il buco nero in San Lorenzo. Privati spartiti, si arena il project per Sant'Orsola niente speranze." *La Repubblica* 13 July: 6.

Wax, Rosalie. 1971. *Doing Fieldwork: Warnings and Advice*. Chicago: University of Chicago Press.

Welch, Evelyn. 2005. *Shopping in the Renaissance: Consumer Cultures in Italy 1400–1600*. New Haven, CT: Yale University Press.

Wertheim, W.F. 1964. "Peasants, Peddlers and Princes in Indonesia: A Review Article." *Pacific Affairs* 37 (3): 307–11. http://dx.doi.org/10.2307/2754978.

Wilk, Sarah. 1986. "Donatello's *Dovizia* as an Image of Florentine Political Propaganda." *Artibus et Historiae* 7 (14): 9–28. http://dx.doi.org/10.2307/1483222.

Zinn, Dorothy. 1994. "The Sengalese Immigrants in Bari. What Happens When the Africans Peer Back." In *International Yearbook of Oral History and Life Stories*, Volume III, ed. Rina Benmayor and Andor Skotnes, 53–68. Oxford: Oxford University Press.

INDEX

Photographs are indicated by page numbers in italics.

Milton Keynes UK
Ingram Content Group UK Ltd.
UKHW012226190424
441406UK00001B/111